Other Kaplan Books for 8ᵗʰ Graders:

High School 411

Grammar Power

Learning Power

Word Power

No-Stress Guide to the 8th Grade MCAS*

Second Edition

*Massachusetts Comprehensive Assessment System

Cynthia and Drew Johnson

Simon & Schuster

SYDNEY · LONDON · SINGAPORE · NEW YORK · TORONTO

Kaplan Books
Published by Simon & Schuster
1230 Avenue of the Americas
New York, NY 10020

For bulk sales to schools, please contact: Order Department, Simon & Schuster, 100 Front Street, Riverside, NJ 08075. Phone: 1-800-223-2336. Fax: 1-800-943-9831.

The material in this book is up to date at the time of publication. However, the Department of Education may have instituted changes in the test after the book was published.

Project Editor: Ruth Baygell

Contributing Editors: Marc Bernstein, Marcy Bullmaster, Phillip Vlahakis

Cover Design: Cheung Tai

Interior Page Design and Layout: Jobim Rose

Production Editor: Maude Spekes

Production Manager: Michael Shevlin

Executive Editor: Del Franz

Manufactured in the United States of America

September 2001

10 9 8 7 6 5 4 3 2 1

ISBN: 0-7432-1415-3

All of the practice questions in this book were created by the authors to illustrate question types. They are not actual test questions. For additional information on the MCAS, visit the Massachusetts Department of Education Web site at www.doe.mass.edu.

Contents

Authors

Cynthia Johnson is the author of several educational books for young people, including *Word Smart Junior* and *Writing Smart Junior*, both of which received the prestigious Parent's Choice Gold Award in 1995, and were included in *Curriculum Administrator* magazine's list of "Top 100" educational products for 1996.

Drew Johnson is the author of *Kidding Around Austin!*, a travel activity book for children, and coauthor of *Kaplan Learning Power*, a guide to improving study skills. Drew is currently an education writer and editor creating workbook, textbook, and World Wide Web–based educational materials for students of all ages.

Welcome to the MCAS

The following manuscript has been translated into English from its original language, Kronhorsti, an alien language spoken by the inhabitants of the fourth planet orbiting the sun Cygnus X-7.

—X!Frumious

TO: The Most Supreme Ruler of the Planet Kronhorst

FROM: X!Frumious the Explorer, currently stationed on Earth

RE: The discovery of standardized tests within the universe

Dear Most Grand Leader of Kronhorst,

Greetings from Earth! As you know, my team of explorers and I have been spending some time on this planet to learn more about its culture and people. For the most part, I can tell you that human beings are intelligent, kind, and helpful, unless you happen to be driving too slowly in the left lane of the highway; then, it's a WHOLE different story, and not one I can tell you with the interplanetary censors around. It is interesting to note that, like every other species we have encountered in the universe, humans have invented the sport which we know as **clickvellsgerstoof** and which they call "professional wrestling." There is, however, one thing that humans have invented that exists nowhere else in known space—standardized testing.

Eager to learn all we could about standardized tests, my crew and I headed our spaceship to our usual landing spot. Unfortunately, the weather was really lousy in the Bermuda Triangle, so we went northwest a bit and landed in Massachusetts. Lucky for us we did, because once there we discovered the **Massachusetts Comprehensive Assessment System**, also known as the **MCAS**. Different forms of this standardized test are given to students in grades 3 through 10. We learned that in 1993, the state of Massachusetts passed the Education Reform Act, a $5 billion piece of legislation aimed at doubling the amount of state money spent on education. Among other things, the Reform Act set high academic standards for students in seven core subject areas, and the MCAS was created to see how well students were learning these subjects. The first wave of students who took this test—the MCAS debuted in 1998—showed the effects of the higher standards. Only 55 percent of all eighth graders passed the English exam, only 31 percent passed the Math exam, and only 28 percent received an acceptable grade on Science & Technology/Engineering. Since then, scores have increased somewhat, but in 2000, most eighth graders were still struggling with these tests. Some critics claim the test was too hard, others that the students are poorly prepared. The debate continues: Every year the MCAS is given, a wave of protests and heated discussion precedes it.

Overview: 8th Grade MCAS

English Language Arts*

	Session 1	1 long composition (0–20 points)
	Sessions 2–5	28–36 multiple-choice questions (1 point each) 4–5 open-response questions (0–4 points each)

Mathematics

	Sessions 1–3	34 multiple-choice and short-answer questions (1 point each) 5–6 open-response questions (0–4 points each)

Science & Technology/Engineering

	Sessions 1–3	26–34 multiple-choice questions (1 point each) 5–6 open-response questions (0–4 points each)

History and Social Science

	Sessions 1–3	26–34 multiple-choice questions (1 point each) 5–6 open-response questions (0–4 points each)

Correct answers needed to pass	Roughly 70% for all sections, although this figure is not fixed
Time given for test	Officially untimed, but designed as 45-minute sessions—extra time alloted within reason
Scoring	Four performance levels: Advanced, Proficient, Needs Improvement, and Warning

*At the time this book was published, the Massachusetts Department of Education was planning to phase out the English Language Arts (ELA) test for grade eight in favor of one for grade seven. However, this may change pending federal legislation. If the No Child Left Behind Act of 2001 passes, every grade from three through eight would be required to administer ELA tests.

The test-taking strategies presented in this book are useful in any grade. So while the content changes for each grade, the way in which you apply tools and strategies remains very much the same.

As you can see, O Great Ruler, the 8th Grade MCAS is much harder than our Kronhorsti test, and the students have fewer brains to help them.

In the spirit of pioneering, I, X!Frumious the Explorer, decided to become the first Kronhorstian to take and pass the 8th Grade MCAS. I put on the regulation human disguise—these Earthlings have only two legs; how can they dance?— and enrolled at Eastbury High School in Somerville. I made some mistakes on the first day I was in school, such as eating a cafeteria bench, but soon I fit right in with the rest of the student body.

After attending some classes, I soon realized that having a college degree from a distant planet doesn't mean you can pass an eighth-grade standardized test. This is because the MCAS was specifically designed by the Massachusetts Department of Education (MDOE) to see how well students were mastering the state's curriculum. Since the MCAS questions mirror the state standards, the test provides a way for the MDOE to determine how well a student has mastered the skill objectives for his or her grade level.

It's a good arrangement, but it meant I was going to need human help if I wanted to pass the test. Fortunately, I found four Eastbury students who asked me to join their study group. It turns out that the phrase "study group" means the same thing in English as it does in Kronhorsti, except in a human study group there's no major surgery involved. This study group already had specialists in the different test-taking areas, but they needed someone to take notes. I eagerly volunteered to be the study group note taker, and everyone was happy.

The members of my study group are:

> **Daniel Bryant**, who specializes in test-taking strategies. He'll also lead our history and social science session.

> **Ridley Anderson**, an expert at mathematics.

> **Angela Lupino**, the English language arts guru.

> **William Walker**, also known as "Willy H_2SO_4," our science whiz. Willy is also in charge of the long composition essay.

> And of course there is me, **X!Frumious**, the group recorder.

O Exalted Ruler, I have provided the notes of our study group meetings on the following pages so that you may learn as much about the 8th Grade MCAS as I have. I have also included MCAS-like questions throughout this book so you can try out your skills on sample problems. It is my belief that anyone who reads these pages, learns the techniques discussed, and uses them will be able to pass this test, regardless of what planet he or she originally came from.

> I Remain Your Humble Citizen,

> *X!Frumious*

> X!Frumious the Explorer, of the planet Kronhorst

Test-Taking Strategies

Session Leader: Daniel Bryant

O Most Mighty One, here are the notes from my first study group meeting. Whenever Daniel wrote something down on the blackboard, I have included that drawing among my notes.
—X!Frumious

NAME: Daniel J. Bryant

BORN: May 22, 1989
Siasconset, Massachusetts

NOTES: Daniel actually likes standardized tests, which puts him in the same category as about one half of one percent of American students. He took the SAT at age 11 for the first time as part of a Duke University study, and he hopes to turn a good score on the PSAT test into a National Honor Society Scholarship to college. Daniel owns one dog, a Malamute named Abacab.

Daniel: First, I would like to thank everyone—Ridley, Angela, Willy, and X!Frumious—for showing up to the meeting on time. Before we start, I asked X!Frumious to go to the store and get us some snacks for the group. How did that go, X!Frumy?

X!Frumious: Just fine, Dan. I was walking down the aisle with barbecue and picnic supplies and I found these delightful items. They really taste great, I think.

Daniel: X!Frumious, that's a sack of charcoal. You're eating gasoline-soaked briquettes.

Ridley: Let's just skip the snacks for now. Agreed?

Strategy 1

Understand the format of the test like the back of your hand. If you know what to expect, you'll feel more confident about your ability to do well. Going into the test with confidence is as important to your success as knowing the specific strategies.

Daniel: Good. Now, down to business. To earn the score that you want on the 8th Grade MCAS, there are several test-taking strategies you'll need to master. The first one sounds very simple, but it's crucial: Get to know the format of the test before test day.

This means you should know how many multiple-choice questions are in each MCAS, how many 4-point, open-response problems are on each subject test, and what the Science & Technology/Engineering section emphasizes.

Willy: Why is this important? We've all taken some form of standardized test before.

Daniel: That might be true, but knowing exactly what's ahead of you on the test-taking days achieves many positive things. First, knowing the format relieves some of the uncertainty about the test, and familiarizing yourself with the different question types should help you avoid becoming rattled or too nervous to do a good job on the test.

Let's face it; since these MCAS tests will show to some degree just how good we are as students, there's a lot of pressure to do well. The normal human reaction is to feel anxious. The problem is, feeling nervous or anxious while you take the test is bound to hurt your score. I don't expect you to be excited about the test, but you do need to reduce any anxiety if you want to do well. One way to do this is to familiarize yourself with the test, so that you can go in knowing what to expect, and what you'll need to do to pass.

Ridley: So Familiarity = Confidence on the MCAS?

Daniel: That's right. But understanding the test format doesn't just help you before the test, it also prevents you from panicking during the test. We all know people who have suffered from "test meltdown," where they come across a question they don't understand and then panic. Under test conditions, a weird question can really affect your focus. By knowing what to expect, you won't get unnerved.

Willy: I'll need an example before I agree with your theory.

Daniel: I'll give you two, Willy. First of all, on the math test, there 5 questions known as short-answer questions. These questions are similar to the math multiple-choice questions, but instead of providing four answer choices for you, the test provides just a blank rectangle into which you must write your answer. It's not a big shift in test format, but if you aren't expecting it, it can still be unsettling.

Then there are the *matrix questions*. Each test section has about 7–11 questions that *don't* count toward your score. These are questions that the Massachusetts Department of Education (MDOE) is trying out for possible use on future exams. While this serves a good purpose— it helps guarantee that your test is similar to the MCAS tests in other years—it also means that roughly one out of seven questions does not affect your score. Some of these questions are easy and others are hard. If you spend 15 minutes on a tough matrix question, then you've just worked yourself up over a problem that means nothing.

Angela: Is there a way to recognize these matrix questions, and then just skip over them?

Daniel: Unfortunately, no. Just don't get frazzled by any one question, because it might not count. And even if that one tough question does count, there's still no need to worry. There are only two real grades on each MCAS test: pass or fail. If you earn a perfect score on a section, you get no special bonus for doing so. So while you should always try your best, this means that no single question is critical to your overall test score. If you're having trouble with a particular problem, don't stress about it.

Information

In every test section, there are 7–11 questions that don't count toward your score. They're called matrix questions because the **Massachusetts Department of Education** (MDOE) is trying them out for possible use on future exams. This means that roughly one out of every seven questions on the test does not affect your score.

The next test-taking strategy is the concept of pacing. Work through the MCAS at an even, steady pace. This means you never rush through a question and make a hurried mistake, but you also don't spend so long on a tough question that you miss the opportunity to answer the easy questions behind it.

Strategy 2

Keep a consistent pace throughout the test. Don't rush through any one question. Even if you think you can answer a question in 10 seconds, remember that the test is designed to challenge you, so seemingly obvious answers may not be what you think. Similarly, don't spend too much time on a question. If you do, you might become drained and lose the focus you need to solve the remaining problems.

You don't want to burn yourself out on any one question. Also, since the tests are administered over a period of days, don't exhaust yourself on the first day at the expense of the other days.

The key to surviving these exams is to maintain a steady pace. Spend at least one minute on each question—if you go faster you may make a careless error—but never more than five minutes. The best way to approach every section is to use a *two-pass system*. Go through each test section two times.

First, complete the easy problems. Then go back and work through the more difficult ones.

Willy: Daniel, you said I should spend at least one minute on every question, but why should I do that if I can figure it out in seconds?

Daniel: Because the test has traps designed to trip you up if you rush. You see, on most tests you take, going fast helps you get to more problems in a limited time. The writers of the MCAS know this, so they've included wrong answer choices that you might carelessly pick if you're in a hurry. Here's an example:

> **Strategy 3**
>
> *Approach every test section using a Two-Pass System.*
>
> - *First, go through and answer all the questions you feel most comfortable with.*
>
> - *When you have finished your first pass, go back through and spend more time on the harder questions.*

1. A teacher is making 7 different walking sticks for use in the school play. If each stick requires $3\frac{3}{4}$ feet of wood, how much wood is needed altogether for the 7 walking sticks?

    A. $10\frac{3}{4}$

    B. $17\frac{1}{2}$

    C. $21\frac{3}{4}$

    D. $26\frac{1}{4}$

Looking at the answer choices, both A and C have $\frac{3}{4}$ in them, and C looks especially good because at first glance, you might think that 7 multiplied by $3\frac{3}{4}$ equals $21\frac{3}{4}$. So if you were rushing through, you'd pick C and rapidly move along.

Ridley: However, if you took a minute to work out the math, you would see that $3\frac{3}{4}$ multiplied by 7 is really $26\frac{1}{4}$, or answer choice D. Initially, this didn't appear a likely answer, but once you take the time to do the math, it is correct.

Daniel: So you see how you can harm your score by going too slow or too fast. Now you all have an idea of how the *two-pass system* works. Let's say you've gone through the first pass, and now you're working on a tougher problem. You spend about five minutes looking it over, but you still don't know how to answer it. Do you leave it blank and move on? The answer is, No, No, No!!

Strategy 4

Answer every question—even if you have to guess. Your score is based on the number of questions that you answer correctly. You are not penalized for wrong answers, so any question you skip is a missed opportunity to earn free points.

You won't lose points for getting a question wrong, so even if you have only a one in four chance of answering it right, make sure to bubble in an oval before you move on to the next question. Any question you skip is a missed opportunity for free points.

Willy: Sounds fine, Dan, but if we have only a one-in-four chance on a question, we won't get many questions right against those odds.

Daniel: That's true, but the next strategy will help you improve those odds. It's called *Process of Elimination*, or *POE*, and on multiple-choice questions, it's an effective way to rule out incorrect answer choices.

Remember, the answer to every MCAS multiple-choice question is right in front of you. You don't have to know it directly off the top of your head, you just have to be able to *select* the answer from a list of possible choices. That means that ruling out clearly wrong answers is just as useful as finding the right answer, because every choice you eliminate brings you closer to getting the problem right. Here's an example of how POE can be effective.

Strategy 5

Use the **Process of Elimination (POE)** to eliminate wrong answer choices. Every wrong answer choice that you rule out brings you closer to finding the right one.

Daniel holds up his right hand clenched in a fist.

2.   What am I holding in my hand?
      A.   a pumpkin
      B.   a penny
      C.   Cape Cod
      D.   an eraser

Which answer choices can you eliminate?

Angela: A and C, because your hand isn't big enough to hold either a pumpkin or Cape Cod.

Daniel: Most observant, Angela. When you come to a question, use common sense to think about what the possible answer could be. The answer above is either B or D, and there's no real way to know which is correct, but having a fifty-fifty chance on a series of MCAS questions means you're bound to get some of them right just by guessing.

> O Mighty Leader, remember your plans to shrink Cape Cod to the size of a peanut? Please cancel those plans; something just came up.

Also, look for traps that might appear in the question. On the math section, one or two wrong answer choices often contain numbers from the original question, or use numbers from the question in a simplified way. These answer choices are usually traps, like in the following example.

3.   Kerry and her mother used 45 feet of rope from a 60-yard bundle of rope. How many feet of rope were left in the bundle?

      A.   15 feet
      B.   60 feet
      C.   105 feet
      D.   135 feet

Before doing the math, if you just think about the problem you can eliminate some answers. Choice B just repeats one of the numbers from the problem above, and it can be eliminated as a trap. If you rush on this problem, you might pick A or C, since these answers just add or subtract the two numbers in the question. However, if you examine the question, you'll see that Kerry and her mother have taken 45 *feet* from a 60

Strategy 6
_____

Use common sense to think about how to answer a question. It sounds simple, and it is, but when placed under high-stakes tests conditions, many students panic and forget certain basics.

yard bundle. That means there's going to be quite a bit of rope left in the bundle, and so choice A is definitely not correct. At this point you can guess between C or D if you can't figure out how to do the math, and since C is probably a trap, D would be your best bet. And it's the right answer.

Angela: But what about the math?

Ridley: Oh, that's easy, you just take 60 yards and multiply by three, so that . . .

Daniel: Ridley could explain the math, but she doesn't have to, because we already have the correct answer, D. This is why the multiple-choice format works so well; it doesn't matter how you get the answer, so long as you bubble in the correct oval. In other words, if Ridley does the math and answers D, or if you use POE to get rid of two choices and then pick D, you both get the same amount of credit.

Of course, you can't use elimination on every MCAS question, like the short-answer or open-response questions, but for multiple-choice questions, it's one of your most effective tools.

Willy: We see it works on math problems, but does POE work well on the other sections?

Daniel: Yes it does. For instance, on the English Language Arts (ELA) section, many *wrong* answer choices are words taken directly from the reading passage. These words have nothing to do with the question being asked, but since you might remember reading them in the passage, and they may indeed be true, the answer choices seem to be correct, or at least reasonable. Consider the following question.

4. Which is a FACT in the passage?
   A. The teachers mentioned in the program are distinguished.
   B. The postal service is very slow.
   C. The skills test will not affect admission into the school.
   D. The school library is open 24 hours a day.

Using common sense, which answer choices can you eliminate?

Ridley: I would get rid of D, since I've never heard of a school library that is open 24 hours a day.

Daniel: So true, Ridley. You can bet, however, that the "school library" is mentioned at least once in the passage, so someone might not cross out D because he or she remembers reading those words in the passage.

Angela: B doesn't seem like a good choice, either. It is such a broad statement that it would be hard to prove as a fact, which is what the question is asking. I would eliminate it as well.

Daniel: Good work, Angela. That leaves A and C, and since A is a general statement that could be hard to prove as well, I would pick C. As it happens, C is the answer. Using only POE, we were able to get the correct answer, and we never laid eyes on the reading passage itself.

POE works just as well on Science & Technology/Engineering (S&T/E), and History and Social Science. Check out the question below.

Use the topographic map to answer question 5.

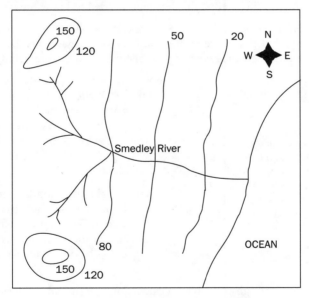

5. The Smedley River flows in what direction?

   A. north
   B. south
   C. east
   D. west

You don't need to be a riverologist—or whatever you call someone who knows about rivers—in order to get this problem right. You just need to look at the map and use some common sense. For instance, the Smedley River crosses the map in a fairly straight line, so what choices can we eliminate first?

Willy: North and south, choices A and B. I can see with my eyes that the river is not going in either of those directions.

Daniel: Exactly. So now, you could either guess or look at the elevation numbers on the map. The higher numbers are on the left side of the page, and since I know water flows downhill, C is the right answer.

Angela: I got C, too, but that's just because I used common sense and knew that rivers always flow into the ocean, not the other way around. So the answer had to be C.

Daniel: You see, you don't always need to know the exact scientific principle to answer the S&T/E questions—often a basic understanding of things will be enough. Here, you needed to know how water works.

For the History & Social Science (H&SS) MCAS, elimination is useful too, but in a more limited way—since many of the H&SS questions require specific knowledge of history. I'll talk more about this later.

Now, the next strategy that you need to know is: Write all of your work down. If you try to solve a problem in your head, you could be sorry later. It just isn't worth the risk, so get in the habit of writing down all of your notes and calculations.

Strategy 7

Write all of your work down, especially on the open-response questions. You will always want to have your notes to refer to, either to catch a mistake or to double-check your work. Don't just work out problems in your head—it just isn't worth the risk.

Once again, this sounds simple, but you would be surprised how many students don't do it. These students feel that they can answer the questions just as easily—or faster—by doing calculations in their head.

Even though you'll have a calculator, you should still write down the numbers on the page first. Why? Because you need to look at your work and decide whether or not you have set up each problem correctly. Do the two numbers really need to be multiplied, or is division required? Questions like this can be answered properly if you show your work, but if you just start crunching numbers on your calculator, you could be making an error unknowingly.

Ridley: But what if the answer is just staring right at me?

Daniel: Then I'd check to see that it's the correct answer, and not just an attractive wrong answer. Think back to the "Bundle of Rope" problem we discussed earlier. Answer choices A and C both looked like great choices if you were in a hurry and didn't do the math. Instead, when you took the time to calculate the math, you found out that both A and C were wrong.

Writing down your work is crucial on the open-response questions. Read the following question and see how Imperious Student A and Well-Behaved Student B respond.

6. Jonathan had $5.00 at the start of the day. At noon, he gave half of his money to Gwendolyn, and at 3:00 P.M. he lost $0.50 in a vending machine. How much money did Jonathan have remaining?

Imperious Student A: Jonathan had two bucks because I say he did. Now all must bow to the brilliance of Student A!

Well-Behaved Student B: Starting out with five, Jonathan gave half, or $2.50 away, so he had three dollars left. Then he lost 50 cents, so $3.00 − $0.50 = $2.50.

Here, Student A has provided the *right solution* with an *inadequate explanation*, earning partial credit. Student B has provided the wrong solution but an almost *correct and thorough explanation*, also earning partial credit. As you can see, the student who got the solution wrong but provided correctly explained the process still earned partial credit. Since one-third or so of your MCAS grade is determined by the open-response questions, showing your work can significantly boost your score.

> *Information*
>
> *For every subject test, students with limited English proficiency will be allowed to use a word-to-word dictionary, provided it doesn't contain definitions.*

X!Frumious: Writing everything down is a very good idea.

Daniel: The last strategy is not a strategy in the typical sense—it's about helping you make the most of your time. If you find yourself getting mentally tired during the test—and that's bound to happen—take a moment to stretch and clear your mind. You don't want to just plod through the test—you want to approach it with a sharp focus. So even though you might be losing a minute or two to rest, you'll actually gain much more than that in the end.

Strategy 8

Take short breaks during the test to help you relieve mental fatigue. If you feel yourself getting tired, just put your pencil down and take a minute to stretch. Stretch your arms, stretch your fingers, clear your mind, and then refocus your thoughts back on the test.

So there are the basic strategies for approaching the test. If you get comfortable with them so that you use them on test day, your scores will improve. But, if you only think about them today, you'll probably forget them.

One more thing. While these strategies can help mentally prepare you for the test, there are some physical preparations you should make as well.

What to Do Right Before the Test

- *On the night before the test, make sure you get enough sleep. Don't go to bed earlier than usual, however. If you do that, you'll probably just lie in bed thinking about the test. Instead, keep your schedule the night before the test as relaxed as possible.*

- *Don't cram for the test. Do a light review and then do something to take your mind off it. Do your studying ahead of time, and not on the last night.*

- *On the day of the test, make sure you have a good breakfast, but not so filling that you find yourself dying for a nap.*

- *On the day of the test, don't take any over-the-counter medication if you don't have to. Having allergies is annoying, but taking medication that muddles your thinking spells trouble for your test score.*

Overview: Test-Taking Strategies

Strategy 1: *Know the format of the test like the back of your hand. That way, you'll have more confidence in your ability to do well. Don't get bogged down or agonize over any one question at the expense of the other questions.*

Strategy 2: *Keep a steady pace throughout the test. Don't rush through any one question or spend too much time on any one question.*

Strategy 3: *On each section of the test, use a **two-pass system**. First, go through and answer all the questions you feel most comfortable with. Then, when you have finished your first pass, go back and spend more time on the harder questions.*

Strategy 4: *Answer every question, even if you need to guess. Don't miss an opportunity for free points.*

Strategy 5: *On multiple-choice questions, use the **Process of Elimination** (POE) to rule out wrong answer choices. Try to narrow down your choices before making a selection.*

Strategy 6: *Use common sense to think about how to answer a question. Watch out for traps in the question.*

Strategy 7: *Write out all of your work. Being able to refer to your calculations on paper will help you more than you realize. On the open-response math questions, you can receive partial credit even if you get a solution wrong.*

Strategy 8: *Take short breaks during the test to help you relieve mental fatigue. Just put your pencil down and take a minute to stretch. Stretch your arms, stretch your fingers, clear your mind, and then refocus your thoughts back on the test.*

Chapter 2

Mathematics

Session Leader: Ridley Anderson

O Munificent Big Guy, what follows are my notes from our second study group meeting, held at the most magnificent place I have ever been in. The place was called a "rec room," and this incredible establishment was located in the basement of Ridley's house, probably for security reasons. I'll tell you more about this place, O Scaly One, when we meet in person.

—X!Frumious

NAME: Ridley L. Anderson

BORN: March 1, 1989
Concord, Massachusetts

NOTES: Ridley was voted Head Cheerleader two years in a row, during which time she instituted a policy of issuing jerseys and numbers to cheerleaders in order to "impose a system of order upon this chaos of pom-poms and hair spray." She then resigned as cheerleader in order to start a mathematics club, and was voted President of Math Club three days later. Ridley owns one pet, a mongoose named Euclid.

Ridley: Hello, I'd like to thank everyone for arriving here on time today. I know that some people find it hard to follow simple directions like "Meet at my house at sixteen seconds past 4:08 p.m."

Daniel: Yes, well, I'd like to take the credit for our punctuality, but we did just follow you home from school. Remember, you said, "Just follow my Mom's car"?

Ridley: Still, it's the thought that counts. Now, my discussion of the Math Section will take 34 minutes, 8 seconds. I would appreciate it, X!Frumious, if you would use a digital stopwatch and notify me at 4 minute, 16 second intervals. Here's a digital watch for you to use. No, X!Frumious, don't eat it.

Overview: Mathematics

Format	Three sessions, each about 45 minutes (The test is untimed, but only "within reason.")
Number of questions	• 29 multiple-choice questions (1 point each) • 5 short-answer questions (1 point each) • 5–6 open-response questions (0-4 points each)
Scoring	Your score is based on the number of questions that you answer correctly. You are not penalized for incorrect answers.
Calculators	Permitted for two of the three sessions

Ridley: *Multiple-choice questions* require you to select the correct answer from a list of four options. Short-answer and open-response questions require you to generate, rather than recognize, a response. For *short-answer questions*, you'll have to provide a short statement or calculations leading up to your solution. For the more involved *open-response questions*, you should provide an in-depth explanation in writing or in the form of a chart, diagram, or graph, as appropriate.

Since this is a math exam, let's do some math and analyze the question type breakdown. On the 2001 8th Grade Math MCAS, there were 29 multiple-choice, 5 short-answer, and 5 open-response questions. According to the value of each, a perfect score on that test totaled 54 points.

Given the question breakdown on the 2001 test, you might think it best to spend more time on the open-response questions, since they're multistep problems that take more time to solve. But, in fact, that's not a wise approach. The multiple-choice and short-answer questions account for 63 percent of the entire test. While the open-response questions take more time, they actually account for less of your grade—about one-third of your score. This is a significant fraction of your score, but not as large as the fraction of your score that is accounted for by the other question formats. With this in mind, you need to remember: Answer all the multiple-choice and short-answer questions first, and leave the open-response questions for last. Spend about 1–3 minutes on every multiple-choice and short-answer question, and then use whatever time you have remaining to tackle the open-response problems.

Daniel: So, using the two-pass system, do I want to make sure to leave the open-response questions for last?

Ridley: Yes. If you don't leave them for last, two things might happen. You might set out to take the test from start to finish, but along the way get caught up and take too much time working a difficult open-response question. If that happens, you'll blow your chance of correctly answering several easier multiple-choice questions that appear later.

> ### Strategy
>
> The best way to approach the math test is to first answer the multiple-choice and short-answer questions, spending about 1–3 minutes on each, and leave the open-response questions for last. Since they account for most of your score, you want to focus your energy on the multiple-choice and short-answer questions.

You might also run into trouble if you rush through the multiple-choice questions in order to have plenty of time for the open-response problems. That would mean you rushed through the majority of test points simply to work on harder problems that are less critical to your score. With both of these scenarios, you'd probably get a lower grade, so avoid them at all costs.

Here's another advantage to answering the multiple-choice questions first: the test-taking strategies we reviewed in chapter 1 work best on multiple-choice questions. If you use them on those questions, you'll be able to earn points with confidence and ease, enabling you to move on to the more difficult questions.

Almost half of all the math answers will be sitting in front of you; all you have to do is select the correct answer. If you don't know the answer, you can always elimininate *clearly wrong* answer choices and then guess. Granted, some of the 1-point questions are short-answer questions, which are immune to POE, but even so, multiple-choice questions outnumber the short-answer questions by a fair amount.

Willy: Should I do all the multiple-choice questions first, and then work the short-answer questions?

Ridley: You could, but you won't gain much by doing so. The multiple-choice and short-answer questions require about the same amout of effort—the main difference between the two is that you can't use elimination on the short-answer questions. So just work these questions in whatever order they appear.

Short-answer problems require you to write out your answer. The format of these questions makes these problems tougher than the multiple-choice. But in terms of difficulty level, these problems are, on average, easier than the multiple-choice. So while you're not provided with four possible answer choices, you're also not being given a real bear of a problem. Consider the following short-answer questions.

1. On the number line, how many units apart are –5 and 3?

2. In the equation below, what does *y* equal?

    $5 + 3y = 26$

Question 1 is fairly straightforward. Think about—or preferably, draw—a number line. This will lead you easily to 8, the answer. In question 2, write down your work.

$$5 + 3y = 26$$
$$-5 \qquad -5$$
$$3y = 21$$
$$\frac{3y}{3} = \frac{21}{3}$$
$$y = 7$$

Once you work through the problem, all that remains is that you place $y = 7$ into the box.

Angela: Pretty cool, but once I finish all the 1-point questions, what should I do about the open-response questions remaining?

Ridley: While the multiple-choice part of the exam is scored by a machine, the open-response questions are scored by teachers who have been given guidelines about what constitutes a 4-

> **Information**
>
> *On the short-answer questions, the format is part of what makes them difficult. Once you become familiar with it, you should find yourself looking at a relatively simple math problem.*

point response, a 3-point response, and so on. To get full credit on these questions, you'll have to provide the solution as well as adequate work that shows you used accurate math skills and not your powerful psychic ability. So, on every open-response question, make sure you show your work.

Angela: What if I come to a 4-point question that I can't answer?

Ridley: If it's hard for you, it's probably tough for a lot of people taking this test. Just move on and answer the other open-response questions. Then, check over your answers in the other parts of the section to make sure you haven't made any careless errors. If you still have time after that, go back to that tough question and give it your best shot. But remember, that one question won't make or break your score.

Strategy

On open-response questions, make sure to show your work, and give every question your best shot. Even if you come up with the wrong solution, you can earn partial credit if you have used sound math skills.

Willy: What kinds of questions are on the test?

Overview: MCAS Math Objectives

Concepts	Description
A: **Number Sense** (roughly 25% of test)	Basic math principles such as fractions, decimals, percents, number lines, and estimation; basic math operations involving real world situations.
B: **Patterns, Relations, and Functions** (roughly 30% of test)	Math concepts based on pattern solving, mainly algebra (using variables) and understanding underlying math functions.
C: **Geometry and Measurement** (roughly 25% of test)	Geometric shapes, principles, and terminology; units of measurement (metric and standard), as well as perimeter, area, volume, time, and temperature.
D: **Statistics and Probability** (roughly 20% of test)	Charts and graphs; probability questions.

Ridley: There are four kinds of questions on the Math MCAS.

But before I discuss those, I want to mention that you'll be given a Math Reference Sheet during the test. This sheet provides information in two categories: *formulas* (for finding the area and perimeter of a circle, and the area and circumference of a triangle); and *conversions* (metric and standard units of length, weight, mass, volume, and time). There is also a ruler, with both standard and metric units. Use the Reference Sheet freely. If you are using the wrong units, having a calculator won't matter.

Angela: That makes sense. I'm not that comfortable with the math anyway, and if I have the opportunity to make sure I'm using the correct formula, I'm definitely going to use it.

Ridley: You got that right. Now, I'll discuss each of the four math sections, and the Objectives that they cover. Everybody ready? X!Frumious, how am I doing for time?

X!Frumious: (*mumbled because of something in mouth*) Delicious!

Ridley: Okay then, here we go.

Concept A: Number Sense

Ridley: These questions test your knowledge of such basic math principles as whole numbers, integers, even and odd numbers, decimals, fractions, ratios, and percents. What makes these concepts difficult is how they are presented. Consider this question.

3. Kaitlyn surveyed a group of people at the mall and asked each person what his or her favorite sport was. The chart below shows the result of her survey. Which list shows the results in order from greatest interest to least interest?

Favorite Sport	Part of Group Surveyed
Soccer	$\frac{1}{10}$
Football	$\frac{9}{20}$
Basketball	$\frac{1}{5}$
Baseball	$\frac{1}{4}$

A. Soccer, Basketball, Baseball, Football
B. Basketball, Soccer, Football, Baseball
C. Football, Baseball, Basketball, Soccer
D. Football, Basketball, Baseball, Soccer

Ridley: This question is interesting because it combines two different number concepts—*fractions* and *greatest to least*. To solve this, let's first look to see which sport is most popular. The best way to do this is to find a common denominator (the lower half of the fraction), for all these fractions. To do this, multiply the numerator and denominator of the soccer fraction by 2, the numerator and denominator of the basketball fraction by 4, and the numerator and denominator of the baseball fraction by 5. That way, all the fractions will have a denominator of 20, the common denominator.

Willy: Once we do that, we see that $\frac{9}{20}$ is the largest fraction there. So, since football is the most popular, I'll eliminate any answer choice that doesn't start with football. That leaves C and D.

Ridley: Which one has more fans, baseball or basketball? Now that we have done the math, we can see that baseball is the answer ($\frac{5}{20}$ over basketball's $\frac{4}{20}$) so we can pick C and move on.

You can see now how the questions on the Math MCAS aren't very straightforward. On question 3, if someone got flustered by the chart format and all the talk about sports, knowing how to get common denominators would not have mattered. Since the MCAS questions are designed to challenge you, be sure to take the time to clarify just what they are asking.

Sometimes POE and a healthy dose of common sense are all that you will need to answer these MCAS questions.

4. Due to increased demand, a car dealership recently raised the price on its new convertibles by 36%. If the original cost of a convertible was $26,935, what is the new cost, after the increase?

   A. $74,819.44
   B. $36,631.60
   C. $26,971.00
   D. $9,696.60

Before you start punching numbers into your calculator, let's think about this problem. If the price has increased, is the answer going to be *greater than* or *less than* the original price?

Daniel: Greater than.

Ridley: Correct. So, we can eliminate D, since this number is way too low. Now, the increase was only 36%, and choice A is almost three times the original price, so we can also eliminate choice A. This leaves B and C, and C isn't much of an increase from the original price, so that leaves B.

Other Number Sense problems are ratio problems. Here, the key is to set up the ratio properly. You will be provided with one complete ratio and will be asked to complete another ratio.

5. The ratio of students to teachers at Middlebrook High is 7 to 4. If there are 28 teachers at the school, how many students are there?

   A. 16
   B. 28
   C. 49
   D. 196

Daniel: I eliminated B because it was a number that appeared in the question. After that, I guessed C, since D seemed too large and A was too small.

X!Frumious: I took the first ratio, $\frac{7}{4}$ and made it equal to the second ratio, $\frac{x}{28}$. Since $\frac{7}{4} = \frac{x}{28}$, the missing number, x, must be 49, answer C.

Ridley: You're both correct. Now, estimation questions are fairly easy to spot, as they usually contain the words *approximately* or *about*.

6. According to a recent poll, about 23% of all students at Brockmorton Junior High School say that they would like to learn astronomy when they go to high school. If there are 815 students at Brockmorton Junior High, which is the best estimate of the number of students who would like to learn astronomy?

   A. 25
   B. 100
   C. 200
   D. 250

Since the word *estimate* appears in the question, you can be sure this is an estimation problem. You need to think about the problem and understand that 23% means about 25%, or one fourth. So

> **Information**
>
> Percent means "out of 100." Therefore, 23% means $\frac{23}{100}$. Estimate that this is close to $\frac{25}{100}$, which is $\frac{1}{4}$, or 1 out of 4.

about one out of four students is interested, and one-fourth of 800 is 200, answer C.

Willy: What if I want to do the math, you know, multiply 0.23 by 815?

Ridley: You can do that, in which case you'd get 187.45, which is closest to 200. However, since you'll have to do some rounding on every estimation question, it's easier to round before you work the math. 800 divided by 4 is much easier than 0.23 multiplied by 815. Estimation questions come in a variety of formats, but they all center around the same thing. Round off the numbers in the problem, work the math, and then look at the answer choices.

Strategy

Estimation questions often require rounding to the closest whole number, closest multiple of 10, or closest multiple of 100. When you round, your total will be reasonably close to the actual amount given in the problem. Make sure you round up or down before you work the math.

An open-response Number Sense concept question might look like the following:

7. Gordon and Eric are playing a game called Guess the Number. Here are some facts:

    Fact A: The number is between 160 and 210.

    Fact B: The number is evenly divisible by 3.

    Fact C: The number is evenly divisible by 4.

    Fact D: The number is evenly divisible by 5.

    Fact E: The number is prime.

    a. If possible, write a number that fits Facts A and B. If it is not possible, tell why.
    b. If possible, write a number that fits Facts A, C, and D. If it is not possible, tell why.
    c. If possible, write a number that fits Facts A, B, C, and D. If it is not possible, tell why.
    d. If possible, write a number that fits Facts A, C, and E. If it is not possible, tell why.

Daniel: Well, they certainly make you work for those 4 points, eh?

Ridley: The question is definitely involved, but if you approach it in multiple steps, you shouldn't get too flustered. In one way, the fact that we are provided with parts a, b, c, and d makes things easier, since we can see the four parts we'll need to answer to earn 1 point each.

Simple trial and error could get you far on this question. Start picking numbers between 160 and 210, and then use your calculator to determine whether or not they're evenly divisible between 3, 4, or 5. However, if you want to get clever, you should start with part c.

Angela: Why is that?

Ridley: Well, look over the question. If you find a number that fits into part c, then you've also found an answer for parts a and b, since they're smaller versions of part c. On your calculator, multiply 3, 4, and 5— what do you get?

Angela: 60.

Ridley: That means 60 and all the multiples of 60 are going to be divisible by 3, 4, and 5. The multiples of 60 are 60, 120, 180—

Daniel: Bingo! 180 fits Facts A–D.

Ridley: Good. Remember, though, we could also have gotten 180 by taking likely numbers and plugging them into the calculator. A fancy approach is fine, but a straightforward attack usually works as well. Don't bust your skull looking for the BEST approach; just think about an approach that will work.

By definition, a prime number is a positive integer greater than 1 whose only two factors are 1 and the integer itself. A number between 160 and 210 which is evenly divisible by 4 is not prime. Therefore, there is no possible number for part d.

Concept B: Patterns, Relations, and Functions

Ridley: This Concept strand contains mostly two types of problems, graph and variable problems. The multiple-choice graph problems, which fall under the Patterns and Functions parts of the Concept, show you a graph, and then check to see if you can read the information correctly. A popular graph problem looks like:

8. Last Friday, Gavin drove his car from his home to a farm outside of town. The graph below shows the relationship between his travel time and the distance he traveled.

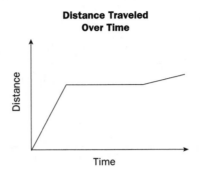

**Distance Traveled
Over Time**

Which of the following best describes his trip?

A. Gavin drove slowly on a dirt road, then on a high-speed highway, and finished his trip on a dirt road.

B. Gavin drove on a high-speed highway, then stopped to have lunch. Afterward, he completed his trip driving slowly on a dirt road.

C. Gavin drove on a high-speed highway, then drove slowly on a dirt road, and finished his trip on a high-speed highway.

D. Gavin drove slowly on a dirt road. He stopped for lunch just before getting on a high-speed highway for the rest of the trip.

Daniel: There's a lot of text here and a graph—this doesn't look like an easy question.

Ridley: It may not look easy, but all you have to do is read the graph and translate it's meaning into words. That's what you have to do on all graph problems. Now, Daniel, the line in this graph has three distinct parts. The middle part is just a horizontal line—how much distance is being traveled in that time?

Daniel: Since the line is flat, I guess there's no distance being traveled.

Ridley: So look at your answer choices and use POE. We need to find an answer choice that has Gavin not moving for the middle portion of his trip.

Angela: In B and D, Gavin "stops for lunch."

Ridley: Good, so we can eliminate A and C. Now we have a fifty-fifty shot if we were to guess. But let's look at the graph again. In the first segment of the graph (the earliest time would be at the left), the line goes up sharply, while in the third segment, it goes up slowly. This means that Gavin was traveling fast in the first segment (since Distance increases sharply), but slowly in the third.

Daniel: So the answer is B, since Gavin's on a high-speed highway at the beginning and on a dirt road at the end.

Ridley: Correct. In question 8, the axes are Distance and Time, and we were able to figure out that a sharp upward line meant *a lot of* Distance in a *short amount of* Time.

Now, if I wanted to make question 8 into an open-response question, I would do the following:

Strategy

When you see a graph on the test, focus on reading the visual information correctly. Pay special attention to how the vertical and horizontal axes are labeled.

9. Last Friday, Gavin drove his car from his home to a farm outside of town. The graph below shows the relationship between his travel time and the distance he traveled.

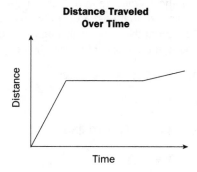

**Distance Traveled
Over Time**

Write a brief story about his trip that accounts for all the changes shown in the graph. Include just enough detail about the different speeds and activities to account for the changes.

You see? It's the same problem, only what makes it a 4-point question is the fact that we now have to explain the changes ourselves.

The other major question type in this Concept strand involves variables and algebra. These questions are often word problems, so be prepared to do reading. Don't be put off by the fact that you'll see lots of text filled with numbers. What you'll have to do is to translate the words into math. You'll probably need more than one step of work to do so.

Don't try to work out these problems in your head, or you'll be asking for trouble. Trying to keep track of all the numbers and calculations without writing them down is like juggling with chainsaws—you might be able to get away with it, but if you slip up, the consequences are very painful.

Angela: But doesn't writing everything down take a lot of time?

Ridley: Not really, because if you get into the habit of writing everything down as you problem solve, you'll be able to do it as quickly as if you did it in your head. Remember, by writing everything down, you eliminate mental errors.

10. Prakash went to an arts show. It cost $4.00 to enter the show. While he was there, Prakash spent money for snacks that cost $1.25 per snack. If Prakash spent $10.25 at the show, which equation could be used to find s, the number of snacks he bought while there?

   A. $4 \times 1.25 \times s = 10.25$

   B. $1.25s + 4 = 10.25$

   C. $4s + 1.25 + 10.25$

   D. $s = \frac{10.25}{4 + 1.25}$

In the above problem, the test makers aren't interested in finding the actual value of s, they just want to see if you know how to find it. This is what I call a "Find the Equation" question. This type of question asks you to find the equation that can be used to find the value of a certain variable.

To solve, we must translate the words of the question into math. To start, Prakash spent $4.00 to enter the show. Then, he spent $1.25 on each snack. Since he bought *s* snacks, the amount he spent on the snacks was ($1.25 per snack) × (*s* snacks), or $1.25*s*. So he spent $4.00 to enter the show and $1.25*s* for the snacks. The total he spent was $4.00 + $1.25*s*, or $(4.00 + 1.25*s*). We know he spent a total of $10.25, so the equation for *s* is $4.00 + 1.25s = 10.25$. This is the same as $1.25s + 4 = 10.25$, which is choice B.

Part of the task on the open-response questions is to come up with proper formulas on your own.

11. Charles is making a display case for his collection of autographed baseballs. In order to keep the baseballs separate, he has placed six wooden pegs, each $\frac{2}{3}$ inches wide, in a display case that is $23\frac{3}{5}$ inches long, as shown below. The space at each end of the rack is the same size as the space between any two adjacent pegs in the display case.

23 ⅗ inches

What is the distance in inches (*x*) between any two pegs in the display case? Show your work or explain in words how to determine the answer.

Unless you dream about variables (like I sometimes do), it's going to take some work to get this question right. Still, it's readily solvable if you remain patient and unflustered.

The key here is to set up the proper formula. The entire display case is $23\frac{3}{5}$ inches long, and it is composed only of pegs and spaces. There are 6 pegs $\frac{2}{3}$ inches long and 7 spaces of unknown width *x*, so our equation looks like

$$6\left(\tfrac{2}{3}\right) + 7x = 23\tfrac{3}{5}$$

Getting the right equation, and explaining why, should get us a point right there. Now it's merely a question of doing the math correctly. In the end, $x = 2\frac{4}{5}$ inches, or 2.8 inches.

Here's another open-response question with variables:

12. The variables q, x, y, and z each represent a different whole number. If you know that $q = 4$, use the properties of whole numbers to determine the numerical value for x, y, and z. Show all of your work.

$$q \times y = q$$
$$z + 2y = q$$
$$z \times x = x$$
$$y + y = z$$

This problem looks tough because you have three unknown variables and four equations, but if you break it down into pieces, it becomes simple. Look at the first equation, $q \times y = q$. Since we know $q = 4$, what number does y have to be?

Willy: It would have to be 1, since the first equation becomes $4y = 4$, so $y = 1$.

Ridley: Right. From there, we can use the fourth equation to figure out z, and z has to be 2 or $(1 + 1)$. At this point, if I've shown my work, I've solved for two of the three unknown variables and have probably earned 2 points. To earn full credit, I would need to see the third equation, $z \times x = x$, which becomes $2x = x$, so $x = 0$.

Concept C: Geometry and Measurement

Ridley: Geometry questions test your knowledge of geometric shapes, principles, and terminology. Measurement questions ask you to switch between different units of measurement. The Reference Chart can help you on some questions, but on other questions, the best technique is something you carry with you at all times: *Your eyes.*

Strategy

The MDOE officially splits Geometry and Measurement into two categories. Since these "combined categories" account for roughly 25 percent of the test, they will be addressed as one concept in this book.

13. A building casts a shadow that is 40 feet long. At the same time Gavin, who is 5 feet tall, casts a shadow that is 8 feet long. How tall is the building?

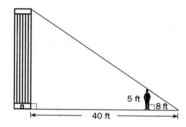

    A.   10 feet
    B.   12 feet
    C.   25 feet
    D.   64 feet

You might believe you have to do the math for this. If you know the math, that's fine, but since this problem is multiple-choice, there is more than one way to find the answer.

Use your eyes and look at the problem. You will see that the diagram is relatively close to scale. If the shadow is 40 feet long, guess how tall the building might be. Is it about half of the shadow, or more than half?

Willy: I say it's a little more than half.

Ridley: Is it longer than the shadow itself?

Daniel: Definitely not.

Ridley: Well, if it's not longer than the shadow itself, that means it is not longer than 40 feet, and we can cross out

> ### Strategy
> *Use your eyes to help you eliminate answer choices on geometry questions that involve lengths of line segments. Look at the diagram that accompanies the question to estimate the correct distance with your eyes.*

choice D. Similarly, if you look at the height of the boy, who is 5 feet tall, and then look at the building, you should see that A and B are too small. That leaves C, so C it is. Don't worry about the math: the real question throughout the test should not be "How do I do the math?" but "How do I answer the question correctly?"

Using your eyes is the key to solving Geometry questions, particularly those involving line segments. Keep in mind, though, that on questions involving angle measurements, the range of answer choices is usually close together, so you won't always be able to rely on your eyes. Try to use the Reference Sheet, too, but that doesn't guarantee success since not all formulas are listed. Watch out for questions that are written in such a way so as to hide the Geometric concept being tested.

14. A rectangular park is 110 yards long and 43 $\frac{2}{3}$ yards wide. If a person walked all the way around the outside edge of the park, how many yards would he walk?

   A. 153 $\frac{2}{3}$ yards

   B. 197 $\frac{1}{3}$ yards

   C. 263 $\frac{2}{3}$ yards

   D. 307 $\frac{1}{3}$ yards

This question asks us to find the perimeter of a rectangle, but in fact, the word *perimeter* doesn't appear in the question! Once you figure out what the question is asking, you'll need to remember the formula for perimeter, which is $P = 2 \, (\ell + w)$—the MCAS Math Reference Sheet does not include this formula—and plug in the numbers from the question. You know that the perimeter is 2(110 yards + 43 $\frac{2}{3}$ yards) = 2(153 $\frac{2}{3}$ yards) = 307 $\frac{1}{3}$ yards, which is choice D.

Daniel: I crossed out A and C, because they both had the fraction $\frac{2}{3}$ in them, and that was the same fraction that was in the original problem.

Ridley: Good use of POE, Dan. Now that you've eliminated A and C, you have a fifty-fifty chance of getting the answer, even if you don't know how to do the math.

Be careful when evaluating answer choices. Dan correctly ruled out the answer choices that had the fraction from the original problem, but this isn't a hard and fast rule. Sometimes the answer *will* have the same fraction as one of the numbers in the question so don't always assume it's incorrect, but it's a good guessing technique.

Two more things you should know about the geometry questions concerns three-dimensional objects and congruency. Congruency, which means same size and shape, is a term that is sometimes used on the Math MCAS. You must also know the basic three-dimensional shapes, such as cubes, spheres, pyramids, and cones. Brush up on what these shapes look like, and you'll be all right.

The open-response Geometry questions sometimes look harder than they really are.

15. A telephone pole, which is danger of falling because of rot, stands 75 feet from a swimming pool. The angle of elevation from the swimming pool to the top of the telephone pole is 50°. If the telephone pole falls, determine whether or not it could hit the pool.

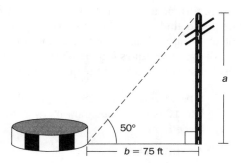

Show your work or explain in words.

Right off the top of my head, I can think of two ways to solve this problem.

1. Use my eyes and take a guess.

2. Use what I know about triangles.

Angela: I'm leaning toward the first method, but I doubt I'd get full credit if I said "The pole could hit the pool because I think it looks like it could."

Ridley: Well, you might get a point if you guess correctly, but I'm going for method 2. You see, we all know that there are 180 degrees in a triangle, right? Well, we have one right angle, which is 90 degrees, and another angle that's 50 degrees. That means the remaining angle is 40 degrees.

Now, the 40 degree angle is opposite the space between the telephone pole and the swimming pool. This space is b. To find out whether or not the pole could hit the pool, I ask myself, "Is a greater than b?" If it is, the pole could make a splash. Since the angle opposite a is greater than the angle opposite b, I think the answer is yes. This is because *the larger the angle, the larger the side of the triangle opposite it.*

> **Information**
>
> Know all the rules and formulas concerning **triangles**, since they are the MCAS test maker's favorite shape.

If there is one geometric figure the MCAS loves, it's the triangle. You'll almost certainly see a question with triangles. You might have to find the missing angle, which is part of what we did in question 15.

As for the "measurement" questions, you'll be asked to do things like find the sum of angles in simple polygons, describe the relationships of the radius, diameter, circumference, and area of circles, develop strategies to find the area of complex shapes, and solve problems involving proportional relationships and units of measurement. For the most part, these questions aren't straightforward, and are written to challenge you. Check out the question below.

16. A piece of rope is 7.25 feet long. If the rope is cut into 10 equal pieces, how many inches long will each piece be?

   A.   8.7 inches
   B.   7.25 inches
   C.   1.45 inches
   D.   0.725 inches

Strategy

When converting units of measurement, be sure to include the units associated with each number.

If you were in a hurry, you might say, "Well, I just divide 7.25 by 10 and get answer D." Punching those numbers into your calculator would confirm that 7.25 divided by 10 is indeed 0.725. But is D the right answer?

Daniel: I don't think so. The key to this problem is not division, but whether or not you get your units of measurement right. Dividing 7.25 feet by 10 gets you 0.725 feet, and all the answer choices are in *inches*. Since there are 12 inches in a foot—I knew this already, but it's also on the Math Reference Sheet—I could multiply 0.725 by 12 and get 8.7 inches, which is the correct answer, A.

Ridley: Very good. You could also rule out B right away, since it merely repeats a number found in the question.

17. For limited distances, a cheetah can run 1,408 feet in 16 seconds. What is the cheetah's speed in feet per seconds?

This problem would be tougher if we were asked for feet per *minute*, because we would have to convert some units. But it asks for feet per *second*, and since we are given 1,408 feet and 16 seconds, we simply need to divide the two numbers and place our answer in the space provided. 88 (feet per second) is the answer.

> O Most Seismopedal One, I later heard that this rate, 88 feet per second, is equal to 60 miles per hour—which is exactly the growth rate of the national Kronhorsti flower, the Berserker Melon. Quite a coincidence, eh?

Concept D: Statistics and Probability

Ridley: The "Statistics" part of Concept D consists of two types of questions involving graphs and charts: simple and advanced. In simple questions, you'll need to *read* a chart correctly. In advanced questions, you'll need to *make* a chart correctly.

As you might expect, the simple graph questions are usually 1-point multiple-choice/short-answer problems, while the advanced questions are 4-point open-response questions. A simple chart problem might look like this:

18. For one week, a clothing store kept track of the number of customers it had during the week. What is the mean number of customers for that five-day period?

Monday	140
Tuesday	90
Wednesday	250
Thursday	140
Friday	70

A.   98
B.   138
C.   140
D.   250

Angela: Ridley, what does *mean* mean?

Ridley: *Mean* means *average*. To find the *mean*, you add up a group of numbers and then divide that sum by however many numbers there are in the group.

On this chart problem, you have to read the information correctly and then perform an operation with it (find the average). Add up the numbers of customers to find the total, 690, and then divide by the number of days, in this case, 5. You get 138, choice B.

Daniel: I got B also, but I used POE. I crossed out C and D because they feature numbers that appeared in the question. Furthermore, if you think about it, choice D is impossible. I mean, how could the *average* number of customers equal 250, the *highest* number of any day? The average would have to be somewhere between the lowest number of customers and the highest number. That leaves only A and B, and I guessed B because it's closer to the middle of all those numbers, and isn't that what an average is all about?

Ridley: Here's a more advanced chart/graph question.

19. For one week, a clothing store kept track of the number of customers it had during the week. The table below shows the number of customers for that five-day period.

Monday	140
Tuesday	90
Wednesday	250
Thursday	140
Friday	70

Part A   On the grid, create a bar graph that shows this information.

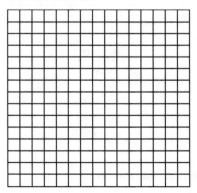

Part B   Complete the circle graph below.

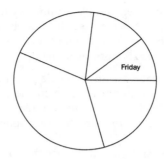

Part C   Determine which graph more clearly shows that over half of the customers arrived on either Wednesday or Thursday. Use the information from both graphs to justify your answer.

_____

_____

_____

_____

_____

Much like the graph problems we dealt with earlier, one of the tricks to doing well on these questions lies in how you label the chart. Once you get this step, the rest of the graph should fall into place. I recommend putting Number of Customers along the vertical axis and Days along the horizontal axis. You can also flip those if you want to.

Once you have labeled the axes, start filling in information. Write in the weekdays, Monday through Friday, along the horizontal axis. As for the vertical axis, what is the greatest number of customers on any day, Willy?

Strategy

On open-response chart questions that require you to make a bar graph, make sure you clearly label the horizontal and vertical axes.

Willy: There are 250 on Wednesday.

Ridley: Right, so when you place numbers along the vertical side, you need to go at least as high as 250. How else can you graph the information properly? I recommend units of 25, so each square up on the vertical axis means 25 more customers.

Correct labeling on the circle graph is also important. You need to process the numbers given in the chart into sections of the circle graph. Friday is given to you. If you find two sections of the chart that looks like they are the exact same size, what days would they be?

Angela: Monday and Thursday, since they both had 140 customers. And the biggest slice would be Wednesday, since it has the most customers of any day.

Ridley: That leaves two slices, and since one of them is labeled Friday, the remaining section has to be Tuesday.

For part C, the best answer is the circle graph, because it shows that the percent of customers on those two days is clearly more than half the circle, and therefore more than half the total number of customers. That last point is tough, eh? Still, if you labeled the bar graph correctly, and filled in the circle graph correctly, you would still get partial credit.

Strategy

When you see a probability question, get into a multiplying mindset.

Let's move on to probability questions. One type of probability question—one that often includes the phrase *how many different*—usually tests whether you can figure out all the different possible arrangements of a group of items. To help you solve these questions, get into a *multiplying* mindset.

20. Auditions for jazz band are scheduled for 11:00 A.M., 12:00 P.M., 1:00 P.M., 2:00 P.M., and 3:00 P.M. on Monday, Tuesday, Thursday, and Friday of next week. How many different audition choices (consisting of one time and one day) are available?

A.   5
B.   16
C.   20
D.   25

To find the whole range of choices, you must multiply the different variables together. In this case the variables are the times and the days.

Willy: Since there are five audition times, and four days, I would multiply 5 × 4 to get 20, choice C.

Ridley: Correct. Once you recognize the *how many different* phrase, things should go smoothly, even if I make the question more difficult, like:

> Auditions for the jazz band are scheduled for 11:00 A.M., 12:00 P.M., 1:00 P.M., 2:00 P.M., and 3:00 P.M. on Monday, Tuesday, Thursday, and Friday of next week, and in rooms 234, 256, and 278. How many audition choices (consisting of one time, one day, and one room) are available?
>
> A.   80
> B.   60
> C.   20
> D.   9

Here, I've added another variable, the three rooms. Still, you solve by multiplying all the variables, in this case 5 × 4 × 3, or five audition times × four days × three rooms = 60, choice B.

And that's all for the Math MCAS! X!Frumious, check the stopwatch I gave you. What numbers do you see?

Daniel: (*peering over X!Frumious's shoulder*) The watch has been mangled somehow, but it still says, "34 minutes, 8 seconds." Exactly as long as you said it would take.

Ridley: Yippee! Hooray! 2, 4, 6, 8, who do we appreciate?

Everyone: Ridley!

Overview: MCAS Math Strategies

Strategy 1: *On open-response questions, show your work. Even if you come up with the wrong solution, you can earn partial credit, as long as you demonstrate that you have used sound math skills.*

Strategy 2: *Estimation questions often require rounding to the closest whole number, closest multiple of 10, or closest multiple of 100. Round up or down before you calculate the math, you'll have a completing the problem.*

Strategy 3: *When you see a graph, to read the visual information carefully. Look to see how the vertical and horizontal axes are labeled.*

Strategy 4: *On word problems, you'll have to translate the words from the problem into the form of an equation or a diagram.*

Strategy 5: *Many geometry questions that involve angles are drawn close to scale. Use your eyes to help you estimate the given distances and to eliminate any answer choices that appear too small or too great.*

Strategy 6: *Problems that ask you to convert one unit of measurement into another are popular on the test. When you write the numbers from a problem down, be sure to include the units that are associated with them.*

Strategy 7: *When you see a probability question, think multiplication.*

English Language Arts: Long Composition

Session Leader: Willy H_2SO_4

> O Your Pookiness, our third meeting was going to be held in Willy's garage, but it seems Willy's parents have asked him to never set foot in the garage again. We held the meeting in Willy's old treehouse instead, which was quite cozy.
> —X!Frumious

NAME: William Bruce Walker, better known as Willy H$_2$SO$_4$

BORN: February 17, 1989
Melrose, Massachusetts

NOTES: A chemistry buff, Willy once made soap from materials he collected on a Boy Scout nature trip into the Berkshire Mountains. He then wrote the essay, "How Cleaning Your Hands at the Top of a Snow-Packed Peak is a Character-Building Experience," which earned him the Best Essay of the Year from his grade school. A garage accident also earned Willy his nickname, although sulfuric acid was not actually used. He owns one pet, a coatimundi named Heisenberg.

Daniel: This treehouse is amazingly decorated. I love the stuffed moose you have in the corner.

Willy: It wasn't easy to get him up the tree, but it was well worth it. I want to bring up a small piano next, but my parents aren't thrilled about the idea.

Let's get down to business, shall we?

There are two components of the MCAS English Language Arts (ELA) test: *Language and Literature*, and *Composition*. The Language and Literature component consists of reading passages followed by related questions. Among other things, you will be asked to describe, analyze, and apply your knowledge of reading comprehension, your understanding of an author's point of view, your ability to compare and contrast related texts, and your use of English grammar. For the Composition com-ponent, you'll be asked to write a long essay. Since there's a lengthy break between this essay and the rest of the ELA test, Angela and I decided we should give the essay its own study session.

Overview: ELA Long Composition

Format	You will write one long essay.
Time	Officially untimed, but expect two 45-minute sections, separated by a short break.
Scoring	Your composition will be given two scores—one for topic development and one for Standard English conventions. The highest possible score is 20.

Willy:

This session is designed to include all parts of the writing process: brainstorming, drafting, writing, and editing. Because it is so comprehensive, it's a 90-minute session, given as two sessions of approximately 45 minutes each. Even though there are no set time limits given on the MCAS, this is the recommended time that you are given.

In session 1, you'll be given a writing prompt (a topic/assignment), that asks you to take a stand on an issue and write a *persuasive* essay. During this time, you'll prepare a draft of your writing. Session 2 is meant for you to develop, write out, and edit your work. This will be your final essay, which is then graded.

The system for grading this essay is a little complicated. Your essay is graded by two readers who assign it one score for *Topic Development* (0–6 points) and one score for its use of *English Conventions* (0–4 points). Therefore, each teacher assigns 0–10 points total. Since there are two graders, the highest possible score for a Long Composition is 20 points. Your essay is evaluated holistically, based on the following categories:

Topic Development (0–6 points awarded by each grader)

Category	General Description
1. Idea Development	How well does the essay present and maintain a clear theme or idea?
2. Organization	Is there a coherent structure to the development of the essay, with a beginning, middle, and end? Are transitions used properly? Is there a conclusion?
3. Details	What is the quality of the details used to support the main idea? Are the details credible, thorough, and elaborate?
4. Language/Style	Does the essay use persuasive and eloquent language?

English Conventions (0–4 points awarded by each grader)

5. Structure	Is proper sentence structure used?
6. Grammar and usage	~~Does words used good?~~ Is the English language used correctly?
7. Mechanics	Are there any capitalization, punctuation, or spelling errors?

Willy: Theoretically, if you write a brilliantly persuasive essay with absolutely awful English, you could get 12 points (6 points from each grader for *Topic Development* and 0 points for *English Conventions*). If you write a totally unconvincing essay with perfect grammar, you could get 8 points.

First and foremost, concentrate on developing your ideas into a strong composition. Worry about perfect grammar later, after you have built a convincing argument. Grammatical and spelling mistakes can be fixed when you edit and proofread your work at the end of part 2. In fact, you'll even *want* to show the graders your progression from *draft* to *finished essay*. If you haven't

fully supported your main idea, though, perfect grammar won't help. So before you worry about grammar usage, pull together a strong argument that includes detailed support of your main idea.

Of course, if you don't have the other objectives down pat, having a strong argument is irrelevant. In other words, if you don't meet Category 1, Idea Development, and you don't present a clear, logical argument in response to the prompt, you're heading for a score of 0. And if don't organize your thoughts (Category 2), but instead just let your hand travel wherever it wants to, that's an essay hovering between 0 and 1. Same thing if you don't use English correctly (Categories 6 and 7).

Angela: What do you mean by "use English correctly"? I'm fortunate to be a foreigner who speaks English well, but I know that I'm an exception, rather than the rule.

Willy: That's true, but the key is to write English well enough to be understood. If you write the sentence "People should not to be out after curfew hours," it won't matter that you have improper verb phrasing in the predicate because the sentence is still understandable. The key is to justify why "people should not to be out after curfew."

Poor grammar won't kill your essay, but poor supporting details will. To illustrate the various levels of detail that a essay could have, look at the chart below:

Level of Detail	Description
Extended response (weakest)	You have linked your main idea to one piece of information, which begins to clarify your meaning.
Somewhat elaborated	You have provided additional information that further clarifies your meaning.
Moderately elaborated	You have clarified your main idea in even greater detail, through the use of additional illustrations, anecdotes, and examples.
Fully elaborated (strongest)	You have provided thorough, clear, and convincing support for your main idea. You provide a logical progression of reasons, use effective transitions, offer substantial and specific support, and use the English language properly.

Willy: Now that you have some idea about the grading and structure behind the essay, let's talk about the essay itself. You will be required to respond to a prompt—a writing assignment—that may or may not be related to a reading passage. The prompt will ask you to write a *persuasive* essay, an essay in which you try to convince the reader of your point of view.

Examples of Persuasive Prompts:

- Some students feel a lot can be learned from watching several hours of television a day. Write a letter to convince your parents that watching TV has a positive, or negative, effect on grades.

- Many adults think that having a curfew helps prevents crime. Write an essay on whether or not you believe a curfew is an effective deterrent to crime.

Here's a sample prompt for us to work on.

Recently the local school board was given control of large plot of land directly behind the school's baseball field. Some members of the Student Council are recommending to the school board that the land should be made into a park.

What is your position concerning this issue? Write a letter to the president of your school board stating your point of view and support it with convincing reasons. Be sure to explain your reasons in detail.

Now, your first consideration is, do you support the park plan or not? Keep in mind that it doesn't matter which side of the argument you take, just how *well* you support your argument.

Ridley: So "I like the park idea" is not the correct answer?

Willy: Right, and "I do not like the park idea" isn't correct, either. There are no correct answers, only well-supported arguments versus poorly supported arguments. So once you have decided which side of the argument you'll support, start planning your essay. The key to any good essay is thorough planning, so don't just start writing frantically. You'll have 45 minutes to create a draft, so use that time to develop an essay that flows smoothly.

> #### Information
>
> *After 2001, the ELA test will be moved from grade 8 to grade 7 (unless the federal government makes testing in grade 8 a requirement). While the essay format will not change, the prompt may ask you to write a descriptive essay, rather than a persuasive one. Many of the strategies presented here can be applied, or adapted to, either type of essay.*

First, brainstorm for ideas. Write out all the reasons you might use to convince the reader of your position. Even if you think something seems offbeat, write it down. You're only brainstorming now, and having some unusual ideas could make your essay engaging and interesting, as long as they support your argument. Keep in mind, though, that you'll want your ideas to connect.

Once you're done listing out your ideas, explain each one in fuller detail. For instance, let's say my main statement is, "I like fresh fruit better than rotten fruit." I should now come up with at least four connected reasons that explain why I like fresh fruit.

Ridley: Four reasons so that you cover the four stages of elaboration you mentioned earlier, right?

Willy: Exactly. If I only said, "I like fresh fruit because it tastes good," then I'd get only an *extended* response, and I'm shooting for *fully elaborated*. Therefore, in my planning stage I would write on a scratch sheet of paper:

<u>Main idea: I like fresh fruit better than rotten fruit.</u>

1. Fresh fruit tastes better than rotten fruit, so I'll probably enjoy it more.
2. Since I enjoy eating fresh fruit, I eat a lot of it, and since it's nutritious, I improve my health by doing so.
3. Rotten fruit could have diseases or bacteria that would make me sick, while with fresh fruit that probably wouldn't happen.
4. Fresh fruit is easier to find, since most stores don't sell rotten fruit (though I could buy fresh fruit and then let it rot, but it would take a while).
5. Some types of rotting fruit eventually become foods of their own, such as grapes changing into raisins, but if I wanted to eat raisins, I'd buy a box of raisins, and if I wanted to eat grapes, I'd buy fresh grapes.

Some reasons will be better than others. Looking over them, reason 1 is good, and the fact that it's linked to reason 2 makes them both valuable to include in the essay. Reason 3 is pretty good, but I should find a way to develop that idea some more. Reasons 4 and 5 are helpful because they show I'm trying to look at both sides of the argument. In reason 5, I take the pro–rotten fruit side and claim that some rotting foods become foods of their own, but then I quickly refute that and reinforce my original idea.

The planning stage is where you make or break your essay, so take the time to come up with as many compelling reasons as you can. If you come up with 10 reasons, pick the most convincing ones and then figure out how they best fit together. Also, get to know your audience. What you would write to one group of people wouldn't necessarily be the same as what you would write to another group. Your language might be *more* (or *less*) formal, and you might choose different vocabulary, depending on whom you need to address.

Let's take the prompt about the proposed park and work through a mock essay. My first question is, "Do I want to support the park idea or not?" In this case, I'm not going to support the Student Council position. I believe an organic vegetable garden would be a better idea for the land. Now that I've decided on my position, I'll brainstorm supporting ideas.

<u>Ideas for Organic Vegetable Garden Essay</u>

1. Offers a variety of unique learning opportunities in both farming and science.

2. Gives students a good reason to be outside on a beautiful day.

3. Sale of vegetables could be used to fund field trips and other activities.

4. Hands-on experience in farming could give students a helpful advantage in summer internships.

5. Vegetable sale can be run as a business, giving people work experience.

6. Students on detention can pick weeds.

7. No other school has an organic vegetable farm, making us stand out.

8. New school mascot: Binky, the additive-free rutabaga.

Now, I'll have to decide on the best sequence to put them in. I may even have to eliminate any ideas that are just too weak or unrealistic for this argument. Once I have my list of ideas, I'll have to organize them in a clear, logical way.

Strategy

After you have brainstormed for ideas, select the best ones and think about how to order, develop, and connect them. Also, think about the audience to whom you are writing and use appropriate language.

Looking them over, I think I can group some of the related points. For instance, I think ideas 1, 4, and 5 are closely connected, since they all relate to using the farm for learning purposes. I could write a paragraph that looks something like this:

> Dear School Board President,
>
> Instead of using the vacant space next to the school for a park, I would like to suggest an alternative use. There are currently numerous parks throughout the city, and while everyone enjoys green spaces, I believe we could do better here at Eastbury High: Let's start an organic vegetable farm.
>
> Having an organic vegetable farm would provide a wealth of learning opportunities for our students. Students in botany could get hands-on experience dealing with plants and seeing how they grow, something that I believe most other high-school students don't get in their schools. Science students could also use the garden to learn more about genetics, as they could combine plants with different characteristics to see what occurs. Students could also eat the vegetables grown in the garden, or even sell them in order to raise money for school activities, like field trips and school dances. If you put students in charge of selling the produce, then they would gain valuable business experience, learning all about the sale and pricing of fruits and vegetables.

I could go on with this paragraph, but I think you get the point. On the real essay I would definitely write more, because the more related points I can string together, the closer my chances are that I reach full elaboration.

Strategy

Always try to present an understanding of both sides of the argument. If you can describe the other side's position, and reasons why you disagree with it, then you'll strengthen your essay.

Daniel: But what about the other ideas? I don't see how you're going to attach the mascot idea to anything.

Willy: Then I won't use it. I don't have to use all of the ideas I first thought of, and if I come up with anything new as I write, I can include that as well.

One other paragraph I should include is the one where I look at the possible objections to having an organic garden, and then reject them one by one. This shows I understand both sides of the argument.

> Some close-minded people might be against the marriage of schools and organic farms. Perhaps they think that learning about farming is pointless, since most students won't farm again after school, and those that do will do so on massive farms that use computerized harvesters and automated sprinklers. To claim that this is a useless exercise would be missing the entire point of education, which is to learn new things. Maybe none of us will become farmers. So what? We can still have gardens of our own when we're older; that way, we can grow our own vegetables, which are almost always superior to those at the store.
>
> Other critics might claim that the idea is "crazy" just because no one has done it before. But what better way to instill a spirit of pride than to do something original? Morale is important for students, and implementing an organic garden would set us apart from other schools. Lastly, having a mascot like "Binky the Additive-free Rutabaga" would accurately represent this project. I know for a fact that our current mascot, the tiger, has never roamed the lands around Eastbury High.

Finally, before you start writing out your essay, there is one last thing you need to bear in mind: penmanship. *If you have poor cursive penmanship, print out your essay.* Make it easy for the graders to read or your essay score will suffer.

> **Strategy**
>
> *Make sure you write neatly. Readers won't grade what they cannot read.*

Any final questions about the essay? Good.

Overview: Writing the Long Composition

- First, brainstorm for ideas. Use numbers to list your points, elaborating on every idea.
- Select your best ideas and decide how to clearly connect them together. Your goal is to persuade your audience of your point of view. Your essay must flow, so use transition words and ideas to link your ideas.
- Use language and tone that are appropriate for your audience.
- Your essay should be 3–4 paragraphs in length. It should contain an introduction, a body, and a conclusion. State your argument and briefly describes the reasons you will provide in support of it. Then, support your reasons with facts and examples. Lastly, conclude by briefly restating your argument and the reasons behind it, using somewhat different language.
- Once you've finished writing your essay, revise and proofread it.
- Neatness counts!—make certain that your handwriting is legible.

Chapter 4

English Language Arts

Session Leader: Angela Lupino

O Most Truculent Czar of the Galaxy, this meeting took place in Angela's room. There were books everywhere! Many were on bookshelves, but others were stacked up from the floor to create teetering, six-foot columns of books. At first, I was sure that I was mere moments away from being brained by the Time Life Series: *Gunfighters of the Wild West* set of books balanced unsteadily near my head, looming like some leather-bound jungle animal in eight easy-to-read volumes. Luckily, no such disaster occurred.

—X!Frumious

NAME: Angela Ines Lupino

BORN: November 27, 1989
Havana, Cuba

NOTES: Angela showed a remarkable ability to read and comprehend at an early stage of life. She finished all the Curious George books by age four, read 10 books of Charles Dickens by age 11, and wrote her first book at age 12, though she has yet to find a publisher willing to print an autobiography of someone who can't even drive. She was voted by classmates as "Most Likely to Write a Thousand-Page Novel While in High School."

Angela: Greetings, everyone, and welcome to my humble room and library. I hope you all are comfortable?

Daniel: Angela, there are books everywhere.

Willy: Where is the floor? I cannot see it. Well, not a lot of it, anyway.

Angela: Trust me, Willy, it's there. What else could the books on my floor be resting on? I know many people think I read too much, although I can tell you right now that such a thing is impossible. There are simply too many good books out there, and no one person could read them all. Speaking of reading, let's talk about the English Language Arts (ELA) MCAS, shall we?

Overview: ELA Sessions 2–5

Format	*6–10 passages*
Number of questions	• *36 multiple-choice questions (1 point each)* • *4 open-response questions (0–4 points)*
Time	*untimed, but 45 minutes alloted for each session: extra time is given "within reason"*
Scoring	*Your score is based on the number of questions that you answer correctly. You are not penalized for incorrect answers.*

Today, we'll talk about what will be included on the *Language and Literature* component of the test. There are three sessions, and you will have approximately 45 minutes for each session. You'll be required to read a passage of text and then answer questions about what you have read. Approximately 5–7 questions follow each passage; most will be multiple-choice, but a few will be open-response, which means you must think about and write out your answer. The open-response questions will take more time to answer, but account for only one fourth of your score. Therefore, leave them for last, after you have done the multiple-choice questions.

Strategy

Do the multiple-choice questions before you attempt the open-response questions. The open-response questions are more time consuming, but account for less of your score, so tackle them last.

This is helpful for two reasons. First, most of us are more comfortable answering multiple-choice questions. And, since they don't take a lot of time, we can work through them quickly and confidently before we delve into the more involved questions. The other reason to do the multiple-choice questions before the open-response questions is that they require different things of you. If you can, it's better to complete a series of same-type questions rather than switch back and forth from one type to another. Otherwise, you might lose your concentration. Multiple-choice questions see how well you can *recognize* an answer in relation to what you have read, while open-response questions test how well you can *generate* an answer in relation to what you have read. Both are tied to the passage, but having to write an answer in your own words makes it a whole different ballgame.

Here's a chart with my pacing suggestions for ELA Sessions 2–4:

For This Activity . . .	Spend This Much Time
Reading a passage	5–7 minutes per passage
Multiple-choice questions	1–2 minutes each
Open-response questions	5–10 minutes each

Daniel: I'm not a fast reader. What if I need more time to read each passage?

Angela: Any time you spend reading takes away from the time you have to answer questions, so I recommend getting through the passage as quickly as possible. Officially, this test is untimed, but you don't want to go at such a leisurely pace that you drag it out. Read the passage to get an idea of what's going on, and then start answering questions. You see, in most of our regular school classes, we learn about a topic and then take a test to see how well we remember what we have learned. But this isn't the best approach for the ELA MCAS. Here, trying to memorize the details from a passage is just a waste of time. Instead, read the text to determine what the main point is, and to get a good idea of what, and where, the facts are. Then, answer the questions, but refer to the passage to check your answers.

Information

The ELA MCAS is an open-book test. You don't need to memorize any information from the reading passages, since you can refer to them at any time. Read a passage to identify the topic or main point, and to get a good idea of what—and where—the facts are. Then, as you answer the questions, go back and reread sections as needed.

Ridley: What if I look back at the passage but can't find the answer to a question?

Angela: Then use POE to eliminate some answer choices, take an educated guess, and move on. You need to get only about 70% of the questions correct to pass, so don't panic over—or spend 10 minutes agonizing over—any one question.

Now let's talk about the passages themselves. The reading passages will average about 800 words each and can be broken down into three categories:

1. Literary (or fiction) passages

2. Informational (or nonfiction) passages

3. Oddball passages

A *literary* (fiction) passage usually tells a story, often about someone our age, and often has an uplifting or inspiring theme. An *informational* (nonfiction) passage is typically educational or instructional, perhaps in the form of a biography or a recollection of a famous event.

The third type is what I call an *oddball* passage, since it comes in a variety of different styles: it might be a letter of recommendation, a poster from a play, or even a page from an instruction manual. Despite its unique format, an Oddball passage should be treated in the same way as are the other passage types.

The most important thing to remember is to *work through the reading passages in whatever order you are comfortable with.* There's no reason you have to start with the first question and end with the last. If you enjoy literary passages, address those first, and then move on to the informational and oddball passages. Of course, if you work out of sequence, you'll have to make sure to fill in the proper answers on the answer key, but that shouldn't be hard to do.

Strategy

- Work through the problems in whatever order you're most comfortable with.

- If you do answer the questions out of sequence, make sure to keep track of your answers.

- Focus first on the passages that have the most questions. Since you'll be fresher at the start of the test, you can confidently get more questions out of the way.

You can also use the number of questions per passage to determine which passages to work first. For instance, if you can start with a short passage with 9 questions or a long passage with 4 questions, you might want to work on the shorter passage first because it takes less time to read and includes more questions. Remember, the goal is to answer questions, not to read passages, so focus first on the passages with the most questions. And since you're fresher at the start of the test, you should use that to your advantage.

Once you realize that you can work through the problems any way you like, you should gain some confidence in your ability to do well.

Before I discuss each question type, let me provide you with a sample reading passage. I think you'll find it is typical of what you'll see on the MCAS.

The Beautiful Summer Day

"Hey, Margaret, why don't you come play softball with us?" asked Margaret's brother Juan. "It's a beautiful day outside." Juan was standing in the doorway holding his bat and two gloves. Behind him his friends Ashok and Joey were waiting on the front steps of the house.

Outside the day was bright and sunny, one of the best days in what had been a very hot summer. Yet even though the beautiful day was tempting, Margaret did not feel like going outside. "Thanks, Juan, but I am just not in the mood to play softball right now. You go on."

"Okay, sister, but school's starting soon, and we won't get many more chances to play softball on a Wednesday afternoon. My friends and I will be at Grompton Park if you want to catch up." Juan picked up a baseball cap and left the house.

Margaret watched her younger brother leave and then let out a deep sigh. Juan was right. School was starting soon, and she should be spending the time before her senior year started to enjoy herself and have some fun. Unfortunately, Margaret was worried about the upcoming year too much to enjoy herself. In some ways, she was excited about the prospect of applying to college, but at the same time it frightened her. What if she did not get into the college of her choice, or any college at all? Margaret hoped to be a music major in college. She knew she was a very good violinist, but music schools were very competitive, and some of them were also fairly expensive. Margaret's parents would help her out financially as much as they could, but Margaret knew she would have to come up with a portion of the money herself. She had worked at her father's office for the first part of the summer, and had earned a little money that way, but the project she had been working on was finished. Margaret knew she would have to find a job during the school year, and although she had worked and gone to school before, it did not leave her with as much free time as she would like.

Margaret went to her room and read for about thirty minutes, but even a book by her favorite author could not help her mood. She went into the study to see if her mother was working on her latest painting, but she was not there. However, there was a slip of paper left on the table addressed to her. Margaret picked up the note and read it:

Dear Margaret,

Someone named Teresa called for you this morning while you were in the shower. She asked you to give her a call at 555-8645. I had to go out and buy some more art supplies, but I should be home by 4:30.

The note was a little puzzling to Margaret at first. She had one friend named Teresa, but she lived in Buffalo, which was over 200 miles away. But since the number Mom wrote down was a local number, that must mean that Teresa was in town. Margaret and Teresa had met during band summer camp two years ago, and quickly became good friends. Teresa was an excellent flute player, and the two of them had even played together on several occasions. Still, Margaret did not go to band summer camp this year, and she had not heard from Teresa in several months.

Margaret dialed the number her Mom had left her. After several rings, a male voice answered, "Hello?"

"Hello, this is Margaret Brantley. May I speak to Teresa?"

"Sure, let me just find her," the man replied. "I think she's in the kitchen with her brother." The line went silent for a while, and then Teresa's voice said, "Margaret? Is that you?"

"It certainly is," she replied. "How are you, Teresa?"

"I'm wonderful!" exclaimed Teresa. "My parents just moved to town, so now I live only a few miles away."

"That's great, Teresa!"

"And there's more," continued Teresa. "My father got the job as the head chef at Bertram's, and they're looking for a group of musicians to play there on the weekends. I asked if I could get the job, and the owner of Bertram's agreed, but only if I could find a quartet. I have a cello player, and a clarinetist, but we need a violinist. Are you interested? It pays very well."

Margaret did not hesitate at all. "You bet I am! What do I need to do?"

Teresa told her. "Our first practice is tomorrow at 10:00. Can you make it?" Margaret told her she could, and Teresa gave Margaret her new address. Then she ended the conversation, claiming that she had to help unpack.

Margaret put the phone down in an exuberant mood. For such a short phone call, it contained a lot of good news. Margaret looked down at her feet and noticed her softball glove lying underneath the kitchen table. She picked it up and headed out the door for Grompton Park. After all, she thought, it would be a shame to waste such a beautiful day.

Multiple-Choice Questions

Angela: There are four types of multiple-choice questions on the ELA test:

- Word Meaning Questions
- Supporting Idea Questions
- Summarization Questions
- Inference and Generalization Questions

Question Type 1: Word Meaning Questions

Angela: Word Meanings questions test your vocabulary. There won't be too many of these questions on the test, but learning the strategies for how to answer them will actually help you on the entire test.

The reading passage will contain a difficult word, like *exuberant*, and a question will ask:

1.   In the passage, the word *exuberant* means—

If you know what the word means already, great. If not, you'll have to figure it out yourself. Remember, you won't have access to a dictionary in this section of the test. The best way to figure out what a word means is to look at how it's used in the sentence, also called context.

X!Frumious: That sounds kind of hard.

Angela: It's easy once you get the hang of it. All of you have learned words in context. Take the sentence, "Maria feigned being sick so she could stay home from school." If you don't know what *feigned* means, you can still figure it out by looking at the rest of the sentence. It means *faked*.

Here's another example. Suppose we heard a phone ringing and I said, "Could you please pick up that *mackinute*? I'm expecting an important call." What do I mean by *mackinute*?

Daniel: I believe you intend for *mackinute* to mean *telephone*.

Angela: Exactly! You figured it out by using clue words like *pick up* and *important call*. Try the problem below, referring back to *The Beautiful Summer Day* passage.

1. In this passage, the word *exuberant* means—

    A. spirited
    B. fretful
    C. disillusioned
    D. capable

Look at the sentence after *exuberant*, and determine what kind of word *exuberant* should be. Is it a positive or negative type of word?

> **Strategy**
>
> There are two ways to get the correct answer on a Word Meaning question:
>
> 1. know the meaning already; or
>
> 2. figure out the meaning of the word from the sentences around it.

Ridley: I would assume it stands for something positive, since Margaret just received all that good news.

Angela: Correct. And if we know *exuberant* will be positive, we can eliminate B and C, both negative words. That leaves A or D, and since Margaret seems happier than efficient, A is the correct choice.

If you like answering these kinds of questions, here's something you can do during the test. Before reading a passage, look to see if there is a Word Meaning question. If there is one, figure out what the word means as soon as you read it, and then go straight to the question to answer it.

Daniel: Yeah, why not? I know the word will show up as a question, so why not answer it as soon as I see it?

Ridley: Oh, no. I prefer reading the entire passage to get the general idea, and then going to the questions. I'm afraid I would lose my train of thought if I left the passage midway through to go answer a question.

Angela: Either way, the choice is yours. Of course, Ridley, when you get to the Word Meaning question, go directly to where it appears in the passage and reread the sentences around it. I recommend starting two sentences before the word, and reading through until two sentences after it, just to make sure you understand the context.

> **Strategy**
>
> When you come across a new word, you might want to figure out what it means right away and go straight to the Word Meaning question to answer it. Start two sentences before the underlined word, and continue through until two sentences after it to determine its meaning.

Learning how to answer Word Meaning questions will help you on the entire ELA test because it trains you to look back at a reading passage. Also, there might be a question that asks about the meaning of an entire phrase or sentence, rather than a specific word, such as, "What did Margaret mean when she said, 'it would be a shame to waste such a beautiful day' at the end of the story?" You would answer this type of question the same way you would approach any Word Meaning question: Read the sentences around it and determine the meaning of the phrase from the context of the story.

Question Type 2: Supporting Idea Questions

Angela: Supporting Idea questions focus on small facts stated within a reading passage—facts you probably wouldn't remember if you read the passage just once and went on to the questions. Answers to these questions are always directly stated in the passage, so the key here is to refer to the passage. Here's a simplified example.

A man in a blue business suit walks into a bank wearing a large green duck on his head. The bank teller looks at him and asks, "Is it hard to keep that thing balanced like that?"

"Not really," replied the duck. "I've got sticky, webbed feet."

O Galactic Uberdude, at first I was puzzled by this story, but then I learned that, unlike us, humans do not usually wear ducks as headgear. (Truly, these humans have no sense of fashion.) I also learned the hard way that Earth ducks are not the well-spoken intellectual philosophers that our Kronhorstian ducks are. However, both duck breeds eat bread crumbs when you throw them some.

Supporting Ideas questions related to the above story would be, "What color was the man's suit?" or "What size was the duck?"

The main pitfall with these questions is when you *sort of* remember an answer, and one of the answer choices looks right, so you pick it. But it's wrong! There's no point in trying to answer these questions from memory; it will only hurt your score. Going back to *The Beautiful Summer Day* passage:

2. In the story, Margaret's mother was not around because she—

   A. went to buy art supplies.
   B. was in the shower.
   C. was at Grompton Park.
   D. went to play softball.

This isn't a central fact in the story, but it is mentioned, so we need to just find where in the passage it is. This is why, when reading the passage for the first time, you try to get a general idea of *what* events occur *when*. If you do that well, you'll head straight to the note that says Mom went to buy art supplies, and you'll see that choice A is correct.

Ridley: Are there any good elimination techniques to use on this question?

Angela: Not many, because on the one hand the answer is taken directly from the passage. You either find it or you don't. On the other hand, if you read that Juan is at Grompton Park and he's playing softball, you could correctly assume that C and D are incorrect answer choices left there to trap you if you confused Juan's actions with his mother's activities. But even if you cross out C and D, it's still in your best interest to look for the precise answer, because it will be there somewhere.

> **Strategy**
>
> *Don't try to answer Supporting Idea questions based on what you think you remember or what looks right. Go back and look at the passage for the precise answer.*

Question Type 3: Summarization Questions

Angela: I started this study group by saying you should first read a passage to get the main idea. Of course this will help you comprehend the passage better, but it will also help you answer Summarization questions. These questions want to know about the main idea or topic of what you have read. So as you read, look for the *big picture*. Figure out what the point of the reading is—what does the author want to communicate? If you are analyzing a literary passage, chances are that the correct answer will be a positive, uplifting message. So when you go to the answer choices, look for the positive answer choice. If you are analyzing an *informational* passage, figure out what the overall message of the text is and identify it in the answer choices.

It may help to understand the individuals who write these reading passages for the MCAS. These people are educational writers who try to write positive, character-building stories for eighth-graders. With this in mind, you probably won't see literary passages that discuss gambling addiction or teenagers dying in a senseless, foreign war. Instead, you'll see biographies of inspirational people, and short stories about students who overcome obstacles and become better people for it. So when you go to select an answer, look for a broad, uplifting answer choice. Let's look at a question from a literary passage none of us have even seen.

2. What is the best summary of this passage?

   A. Joy and her mother use a wooden cage baited with chicken to catch a large opossum.
   B. Despite the difficulties presented by Morris, Joy and her mother decide to still pick berries in the nearby field.
   C. Joy believes the large and cunning Morris may be the same opossum that Joy's mother once tried to catch.
   D. Although their efforts to catch the opossum fail, Joy develops a deep respect for the animal and gains more respect for her mother's spirit and endurance.

We know nothing about the passage itself, but we do know about the writers of the test, so here's how to answer this question. First, A and B might indeed be facts in the passage, but they're really details, not main ideas. Also, neither one is particularly uplifting. Same thing for C. Choice D, however, has a broad message that communicates the warmth that the characters feel for each other. It's the correct response.

> ### Strategy
>
> To answer a Summarization question, read the passage and state the main idea or topic in your own words. Look for the answer choice that captures that main idea or topic. Watch out for answer choices that may be small details in the passage—you may have read about them, and they may indeed be true—but they're not summary statements.

Hopefully, you already suspected that the main idea of the passage had something to do with Joy and her mom sharing a bonding experience, which would make D all the more obvious choice. Now let's try a question from *The Beautiful Summer Day* passage.

3. What is the best summary of this passage?

   A. Margaret's chances for attending college improve after she receives a job offer, leading her to regain her optimism about the future.
   B. Margaret's ability as a musician leads a local restaurant manager to ask her to play at the restaurant.
   C. Margaret knows she will have to do well in school in order to succeed in her goal of going to college.
   D. Worried about having a lack of funds, Margaret initially turns down her brother's offer to play softball at the park.

X!Frumious: Well, B isn't even accurate, so it should go. C and D are both true, but neither one is really positive, so I picked A, which is uplifting. Also, I felt that the point of the passage was something like, "Margaret starts out bumming that she doesn't have a job, but then gets in a better mood because her friend lands her one." Choice A is a good paraphrase of that idea.

Angela: Correct! The test may also include some questions that ask about the main idea of a smaller chunk of text, such as one or two paragraphs. Solve these the same way as you would the other Summarization questions—identify the main point of that paragraph, and look for the positive answer choice.

Question Type 4: Inference and Generalization Questions

Angela: Inference and Generalization questions ask you to draw a conclusion based on information you have read—in other words, to infer something about what you have read. This means that you won't be able to precisely locate these answers in the passage. You'll still need to refer to the text in order to "read between the lines," just don't expect the answer to be obvious.

Supporting Idea question:

1. In the story, Margaret's mother was not around because she—

    A. went to buy art supplies
    B. was in the shower
    C. was at Grompton Park
    D. went to play softball

Inference question on the same topic:

2. When Margaret's mother left the house, the place that she will most likely visit is—

    A. Grompton Park
    B. Teresa's house
    C. Bertram's Restaurant
    D. a painting and crafts store

Since Inference questions don't ask for information directly spelled out in the passage, they often contain words and phrases like *most likely*, *probably*, *might*, or *suggests*. In question 2 above, there's no way to know where Margaret's mother will go, so the question must contain the phrase *will most likely.*

Daniel: That would be D, since you can *most likely* buy art supplies at a painting and crafts store.

Angela: Right. These question types aren't harder than others, they just require an extra step of work. In fact, you can still use POE on them. Think of these questions as two-step questions. First, find the clue, and then, apply it to the answer choices to find the right response. In *The Beautiful Summer Day*, Margaret's mom doesn't state exactly where she is going, but she leaves the house to go buy *art supplies*. If we know she needs art supplies (Step 1), (Step 2) will be to pick the appropriate answer choice.

7. The author of this passage suggests that the writings and accomplishments of W. E. B. Du Bois will probably be—

   A. awarded national honors.
   B. not very useful to future scholars of African American history.
   C. meaningful to future generations.
   D. disregarded by modern human rights organizations.

Daniel: I would get rid of B and D, since they are both negative.

Angela: That leaves A and C, and from there it's a fifty-fifty guess unless you look back into the passage. Of course, since there is no passage, I'd pick C, since it is vaguer and therefore harder to disprove.

Most of the questions on the ELA test are Inference questions. That makes the MCAS a fairly involved test. Inference questions are more time consuming than other question types in that you must identify a clue that will help you answer a question. This would be a much simpler test if these were all Supporting Ideas questions, but that's not the case. Look at this question about *The Beautiful Summer Day*:

8. The author of this passage gives you reason to believe that Margaret—

   A. enjoys playing the violin.
   B. has many friends her own age.
   C. is still working for her father.
   D. plays softball with her brother every week.

Sometimes, it's easier to find all the incorrect answers instead of the one correct answer. That means we'll have to look at the passage to check these answers. We don't know that Margaret has *many* friends, so B can be crossed out. And while Juan asks her to play softball once, there is nothing that states this is a weekly occurrence, so D is out. C is wrong because the passage states that Margaret is no longer working at Pop's office. That leaves A, which I'll pick.

> **Information**
>
> Inference questions ask you to draw conclusions based on information you have read. Look for clues in the question to help you determine the answer. Remember, the answer won't be spelled out in the text. The key is to look for the clue that will help you answer the question.

In fact, there are various indications that suggest Margaret enjoys playing the violin. There's the fact that she wants to be a music major, and her eagerness to play violin with Teresa at the restaurant.

Occasionally an Inference question will ask you about the intentions of the author or the emotional state of one of the characters. Look at the question below, from *The Beautiful Summer Day*.

9. In the first paragraph, the author establishes a mood of—

   A. anxiety
   B. remorse
   C. anger
   D. anticipation

Most of the time, these answers will be positive ones, which means B and C are unlikely to be correct. The reason for this is simple. With these uplifting themes we discussed earlier, there's little room for characters who are *vicious, hateful*, or *irrational*. Therefore, if you had a question with the following answer choices, picking choice D is a safe bet.

   A. vicious
   B. hateful
   C. irrational
   D. agreeable

It still helps to check your work with the passage. Is Margaret in a good mood when the story begins?

Ridley: Not really.

Angela: Exactly. So if this question asked you to describe Margaret's mood at the beginning of the story, you wouldn't be looking for a positive answer. Because of this, if we look at question 9, the answer is A, since Margaret is anxious about her future. So it pays to check with the passage, but just bear in mind that most of the time the warm, fuzzy choice is correct.

Open-Response Questions

Angela: Open-response questions differ from multiple-choice questions in that they require you to *create*, not *recognize/select*, a response. Here, you'll need to write out lots of ideas in your own words, and there's no way to get around it. To answer these questions effectively, you must back them up with details and examples. Your answer might not be thorough enough to earn the maximum number of points, but if you have provided information from the passage in a fairly accurate manner, you should earn partial credit.

> **Strategy**
>
> Back up every open-response question with details and examples from the passage. If you have provided at least some supporting information in an accurate and thoughtful manner, you should earn at least partial credit.

Here are two sample open-response questions for *The Beautiful Summer Day*.

10. At first, Margaret does not want to play softball, but then she does. What makes her change her mind? Use details and information from the story to support your answer.

11. At the beginning of the story, Margaret is excited about college, but she is also nervous. Why is she nervous about something she wants to do? Do you think her feelings change by the end of the story? Use details and information from the story to support your answer.

On question 10, you would need to write 2–6 sentences describing what made Margaret change her mind. Mention her phone call with Teresa, and what finding a music-related job did for her attitude.

For question 11, you might use similar details. Shoot for about 6–10 sentences that describe why Margaret is nervous about college—it's very competitive (fear of failure) and expensive. If you want to quote directly from the passage, you could, but paraphrasing things into your words shows that you actually thought about the question. Finish up by explaining how Teresa's phone call helped ease Margaret's nervousness.

Willy: You mean something like, "The phone call helped Margaret because not only did she get a job, but it was a musical gig, which meant it would improve her chances of getting into music school"?

Angela: Excellent, Willy. One final note. You might see two reading passages in a row, followed by questions. The passages are linked together because they have similar topics. When you're asked about these passages, you will be asked to compare or contrast both of these passages. Make sure you use details from BOTH passages.

That's all I have to say about the ELA MCAS. Now, let's move on to more important business. Who has a date to the Spring Ball?

Ridley: Oh yes, that reminds me. Daniel, I think I need some extra help on the Inference questions: will you help me?

Daniel: Uh, yeah, um, you know, yeah, sure . . . um, yeah.

O Most Viscous One, since I already had a date to the Spring Ball, I stopped taking notes. I was going with the captain of the women's volleyball team, and I even set Willy up on a blind date with Griselda Model 45C, the female android we brought with us from Kronhorst. Granted, as an android Griselda hates most forms of organic life, but it turns out she really likes to dance.

Overview: English Language Arts Test Strategies

Strategy 1: *The ELA MCAS is an open-book test, so there is no need to memorize anything.*

Strategy 2: *As you work through a reading passage, try to identify the main point. Also make mental notes about what and where details are.*

Strategy 3: *Work through the problems in whatever order YOU are most comfortable with. If you do answer the questions out of sequence, though, don't forget to fill in the proper ovals.*

Strategy 4: *Try focusing first on the reading passages that have the most questions. Since you are fresher at the start of the test, you'll get more questions out of the way.*

Strategy 5: *If you don't know the meaning of a word, try to define it by its context, that is, the words and sentences around it.*

Strategy 6: *When identifying the main point of a reading passage, look for a broad, positive-sounding answer. Don't be misled by supporting details.*

Strategy 7: *On inference questions, look for clues that will help you identify the answer. Examine how the question is phrased.*

Chapter 5

Science & Technology/ Engineering

Session Leader: Willy H_2SO_4

> O Most Calibrated One, our fifth meeting was back at Willy's treehouse. At first, I was going to skip this meeting, since what more do I need to know about science & technology? I mean, I have a spaceship capable of interstellar travel, and I know all there is to know about Squarcinos—the gregarious, fun-loving subatomic particles that make up all matter in the universe. Well, then I found out that Squarcinos were NOT going to be on the MCAS, as earthlings are still enamored of such outdated concepts as "mass," "time," "gravity," and even "sound." How quaint!
>
> —X!Frumious

NAME: Willy H$_2$SO$_4$

ADDITIONAL NOTES: With the exception of the Sulfuric-Acid-in-the-Garage Fiasco of '97, Willy's scientific career has been filled with achievements. Recent experiments have included: building an all-plastic aquarium; a report on the comparative density levels of the Eastbury Chess Club and the Football team; and the Moose-a-Pult, a device designed to hurl stuffed wildlife great distances for purposes of entertainment.

Willy: Ah, the world of science. A world of cool logic, precise calculations, and fascinating discoveries. What could be better than that?

Angela: How about a world of *free money*?

Ridley: Or a world of *world peace*?

X!Frumious: Or a world of *fruit-chewy morsels*?

Daniel: Better yet, a world where *everyone thinks Daniel is totally the best*?

Willy: Those are all fine options, and when there's a section of the MCAS that deals with fruit-chewy morsels, I'll be happy to learn all about it. Until then, let's deal with what's on the test.

Overview: Science and Technology/Engineering

Format Three sessions, each about 45 minutes

Number of questions
- 26–41 multiple-choice questions (1 point each)
- 4–6 open-response questions (0–4 points each)

Note: The MDOE is planning to test out many new questions in 2001 and 2002, and a majority of the S&T/E questions will likely be matrix questions. As planned, approximately 57 percent of the test will not count toward your score.

Willy: There are two question types on this section of the test: multiple-choice and open-response. As is the case with the other subject tests, the multiple-choice questions comprise most of your score (two-thirds to be exact), so spend more time on those. As for the open-response questions, make sure to show your work using sound science skills.

The S&T/E test targets four curriculum strands: *Physical Science; Life Science; Earth & Space Science; and Technology/Engineering.* Within the context of each topic area, there is great emphasis on the importance of *Inquiry and Experimentation.* This is intended to help you understand that in science, *what* is known does not stand separate from *how* it is known.

Overview: MCAS Science & Technology/Engineering Standards

Content Area	Percentage of Questions on the Test
Physical Science	25% of test
Life Science	25% of test
Earth and Space Science	25% of test
Technology/Engineering	25% of test

Ridley: It looks like the test emphasizes science, as it has 75% of all the questions devoted to it. Technology makes up only 25% of the test.

Willy: Right. So it would be wise to spend more time brushing up on your knowledge of science than on your knowledge of technology.

Angela: So if I have a choice between looking over a biology book or a book on how to build cars, I should go with the biology book.

Strategy

Since many more MCAS questions will ask about science than they do about technology, spend more study time brushing up on science basics.

Willy: That's correct. Besides, none of us is old enough to drive, anyway.

Let me briefly mention the Process of Elimination here. Using your head on this test can take you a long way, so try not to get flustered in the belief that you need some special knowledge of science. Consider a question that asks about *shadows*. Do you need schooling in optics to know that the longest shadows occur when the sun is lowest, and that shadows are shortest when the sun is high?

Ridley: No, I know that fact from experience. Football practice sometimes ran late, and as the sun set, my cheerleading shadow was about 30 feet long.

Willy: So you see that you don't always need to know about optics to answer the following question.

1. A person is standing in an open field during a bright day in the summer. Sunrise is at 6:43 A.M. that day, while sunset is at 8:52 P.M. At what time will this person's shadow be the longest?

    A.   7:42 A.M.
    B.   9:02 P.M.
    C.   1:04 A.M.
    D.   1:04 P.M.

Ridley: B and C can be ruled out because the sun won't even be out. That leaves A and D. With D, the sun should be almost overhead, so it won't cast much of a shadow. That leaves A.

Willy: Good job. On S&T/E questions, your common sense will come in handy more than you think. More than likely, you'll know some basic scientific principles, though you may not have thought of them in precise, scientific terms in the past.

Since there's an emphasis on Inquiry in this subject test, you'll almost certainly be asked about experiments. For instance:

2. Jonas wants to find out if the rainfall in his town is becoming acid rain. The best way for Jonas to collect this information would be to:

    A.   gather one sample on one rainy day.
    B.   gather one sample on several rainy days.
    C.   gather several samples on one rainy day.
    D.   gather several samples on several rainy days.

Open-response questions will go a step further and ask you to explain how to set up the experiment. For instance:

> 3. Jennifer made several small parachutes by cutting out different-sized triangles of cloth and tying string to the three corners that were in turn tied to one or more pens. She then held each parachute 3 meters above the ground, dropped it, and measured the time it took to fall to the ground.
>
> a. Identify one factor that would affect the time of a parachute's fall.
> b. Predict the relationship between the factor you identified and the time of fall.
> c. Describe an experiment you could try that would test your prediction.

To answer these questions completely, you'll need to have a good idea of the best way to run an experiment. Here are some pointers in that area:

1. *In any experiment, you want to be able to isolate one factor by keeping all other factors constant.* (The Latin term for this is *ceteris paribum*, meaning "all other things equal.") That way, you can be certain that any changes that occur are because of the one factor you have isolated.

Angela: So in question 3, if I want to test how the size of the parachute affects its rate of fall, I would make sure to keep the weight (the number of pens) equal.

Willy: Yes, and if possible, you would want the cloth to be the same material, the wind to be the same speed, the temperature to be equal for each time—ideally, all factors *other than* parachute size should be constant each time.

2. *The more relevant data you can collect* (over a longer period of time), *the better.*

Daniel: On question 2, then, the best answer is D, since Jonas would have the largest amount of samples with that answer choice.

Willy: Right. The more information you have, the better you can prove an experiment. For instance, if Jonas had only one rain sample, who's to say there couldn't be something strange about that sample? Or if he had several samples from only one day, perhaps something occurred that day to throw his readings off. However, if he has numerous samples over a period of time, and they all show the same thing, then Jonas can make a more accurate prediction.

3. *For some experiments, using a control group allows you to judge the effects of an introduced variable.*

A control group is often a way to ensure point 1, *ceteris paribum*. Let's say we wanted to prove that ketchup helps tomato plants grow. To set up a proper experiment, we would start out with two identical tomato plants in identical surroundings (soil, light, and so forth). Then, we would add ketchup to one of the plants, and judge its rate of growth against the plant that doesn't get ketchup. The plant that doesn't get ketchup is the control group.

Ridley: I get it. If we didn't have a control group plant, then there would be no way to know exactly what effect ketchup has on the tomato plant. Sure, it could grow 10 inches, but we wouldn't know exactly what caused it to grow. But with a control plant that grew 8 inches, and a ketchup-fed plant that grew 10 inches, you could conclude that ketchup caused the plant to grow an extra 2 inches.

Willy: Right. Be sure you know how to set up an experiment, because the odds are excellent there will be one open-response question asking you to do just that.

Also, you might be asked to read data in a chart or graph. If this seems familiar to you, it should, since these questions are exactly like the chart questions in the Math MCAS. So you see how learning a technique on one MCAS can often help you on another MCAS. Now, let's go over the specific content areas.

Physical Sciences

Willy: Physical Science questions deal with the world around us. They ask about electricity, heat, gravity, sunlight, evaporation, and how light waves travel. While it's a good idea to have a basic understanding of these concepts, don't worry about having the precise scientific knowledge. Do the best you can with your common sense.

4. Lime juice has a pH lower than 7, is corrosive, and tastes sour. Lime juice is classified as

   A. an element.
   B. an acid.
   C. a base.
   D. More information is needed to classify lime juice.

You don't need to know what "pH lower than 7" means in order to get this question right. Granted, if you do, the question is fairly simple, but if you don't, we can still find the answer. Any ideas?

Daniel: I eliminated A, since I know what an element is, as well as D, since that's the kind of answer anyone who didn't understand the question would pick. That leaves B and C.

> **Strategy**
>
> *While there is usually a precise, scientific explanation for the S&T questions, simply understanding the basic scientific principles and applying common sense often works just as well.*

Angela: I picked B because the question says lime juice is "corrosive," and I know that acids eat away, or corrode, things.

Ridley: I picked B because I read the label of some limeade drink, and it said one of the main ingredients is "citric acid."

Willy: B is right, for all those reasons. Those were some good guesses. Here's another question.

6. A laser beam shines on a mirror at the angle shown below. Which diagram shows what will happen to the beam after it strikes the mirror?

A.

B.

C.

D.

Ooh, lasers! What happens when light strikes a mirror—does it go through it?

Daniel: Uh, no.

Willy: Then A is wrong. So now, let's just decide which answer choice looks like the best answer. Think about how, when you throw a ball at a wall, it bounces off at the opposite angle. That principle would probably hold up on this question as well.

Daniel: Then the answer is D.

Life Science

Willy: Life Science questions examine how well you know the traits and habits of animals and plants. Do you understand a basic food chain, in which the little guys get eaten by the big guys? If so, you'll do well in this section, or in corporate finance. You'll probably be asked about *heredity* and *photosynthesis*, as in the following questions.

7.   Brown eyes are dominant over green eyes in human beings. Therefore, if a pure brown-eyed man has a child with a pure green-eyed women, what color will the child's eyes be?

A.   definitely blue
B.   definitely brown
C.   probably brown but perhaps blue
D.   probably blue but perhaps brown

Information

Key Genetic Points:

1. *Purely dominant traits always beat out recessive traits.*

2. *When two people with a pure recessive trait have a child, that child will definitely have the same recessive trait.*

3. *When mixed dominant and recessive traits are combined, it's anyone's guess how things will turn out.*

If you were to guess, you might want to guess C, since it hedges your bet. Sure, it's probably brown, but why not leave yourself an "out"? But in genetics, that doesn't happen. The answer is B—the child will definitely be brown-eyed.

As for *photosynthesis*, that's the process in which plants use chlorophyll to convert sunlight into energy.

Angela: Chlorophyll is the substance that makes plants green, right?

Willy: I see you've been watching your informative after-school specials, Angela. The main point about photo-synthesis is that if you don't

Technology/Engineering*

give plants sunlight, they die, which is why that fern that Daniel keeps in his sock drawer is quite dead.

Daniel: Oh. I thought it was my smelly socks.

Willy: Using your newfound knowledge of photosynthesis, Daniel, check out the open-response question below.

> **Information**
>
> *In question 7, even though the child will definitely be brown-eyed, he or she will carry the recessive green-eyed gene from his mother. That means that if he or she were to marry someone with brown eyes (but with a recessive green-eyed gene as well), there would be a 25% chance that their child would have green eyes.*

8. You have decided to grow a rubber tree. You must decide where to plant the tree in order for it to have the best growing conditions. Here are the three places you can place the plant.

   a. in the middle of the front yard
   b. next to the side of the house where the garage is
   c. in a large pot near the window of the study

   What additional information would help you decide where to put the plant? Explain why this new information would be helpful.

This might not look like a photosynthesis question at first, but if you don't mention the amount of sunlight somewhere in your answer, you won't earn a lot of points.

Angela: You know, it seems kind of like an experiment—you know, find the best place to grow this rubber tree?

Willy: As you can see, this Life Sciences question takes an Inquiry approach. To solve this open-response question, then, we want to come up with as many variables as we can—amount of sunlight, quality of soil, amount of rainfall, whether or not there are rubber-tree-eating animals inside or outside the house—before we decide on one of the three locations. In fact, the real question is not "Which site is best for this plant?" but "Can you figure out all the variables that go into growing a plant?" If you can answer that question thoroughly, you'll do well on this question.

KAPLAN 85

Earth and Space Science

Willy: There are only two objects you need to know in order to ace this section: the earth, and the galaxy. Earth Science questions talk about minerals, the composition of soil, volcanoes, fossils, and other things that make up our little blue planet. Still, you don't need to be a vulcanologist to know that lava is hot, so use common sense whenever you can.

9. Earthquakes are most commonly associated with—
   A. faults in the earth's crust
   B. volcanoes
   C. soil erosion
   D. rivers and tributaries

On a question like this, you should be thankful for the multiple-choice format. POE should help you here. For instance, D has nothing to do with the inner workings of the earth, so it can be eliminated.

Daniel: You know, I remember watching the movie *Superman*, and it kept talking about doing something to the San Andreas Fault in order to trigger an earthquake. I'll pick A.

Willy: Cinematic knowledge aside, it would be difficult to figure out how exactly how soil erosion or volcanoes could start an earthquake, if you didn't know the science of it. So, I would guess A.

10. Vancouver, British Columbia, and International Falls, Minnesota, are located at about the same latitude. Yet the average winter temperature in Vancouver is 4 degrees Celsius, while the average winter temperature in International Falls is –14 degrees Celsius. What are some of the factors to explain this difference?

This question presents a common theme in this content area, which is the relationship between water and temperature. The S&T/E MCAS will test you on the interconnectedness of various

things. In Life Sciences, it's the cycles of organisms. In Earth Sciences, it's the relationship between air-water-sunlight-earth. These questions want you to understand how rain falling in Nebraska ends up in a river, which flows to the ocean, and how once in the ocean, the water evaporates and ends up raining down on Nebraska again.

Angela: So besides water and temperature, what else would account for the temperature difference?

Willy: Think about the air-water-sunlight cycle. The two cities are at the same latitude, so sunlight isn't a factor. But International Falls might get more Arctic air, and that would certainly lower its temperature. Also, if International Falls is higher above sea level than Vancouver, then it would be colder for that reason as well.

Strategy

For S&T/E questions about the environment and the Earth, make sure you think about the Big Picture (all events connected to a single planet, our own.)

Technology/Engineering

Willy: In this category, there will likely be an open-response question that asks you to explain how to design something. The best way to do this is to present a multistep process. This kind of question would be worth 4 points, so remember the Mousetrap Rule: *There is never just one perfect way to design a tool or object.* If the tool does the task it needs to do, then it works.

You see, you can always build a better mousetrap, but on Design Process questions, you only have to design a mousetrap that will get the job done.

11. Design a two-person tent to be used for a five-day trek in the Hoosac Range.

   a. Describe three physical properties that the material used to construct the tent must have.
   b. Why are these properties important?
   c. Generate a design sketch of the tent and its components.

The first step is to brainstorm what properties your tent should have.

Ridley: It should be windproof, waterproof, temperature proof, lightweight, and have an awesome color scheme. And it should have one of those tiny refrigerators in it, too, so after a long hike, we can kick back with some *Raspberry Fanta*.

Willy: (*Pause*) OK, Ridley. Good brainstorming, but when you narrow your list to three properties, I'd skip the fridge.

Other technology questions ask you to choose the right tool for the job. Know basic tools (levers, wheels) and some scientific tools like microscopes, and you'll do fine. Here's a theoretical question:

12. Which of the following would you use to weigh an elephant?

   A. a postage scale
   B. a bathroom scale
   C. a tiny scale used to weigh diamonds
   D. a truck stop scale

If you picked D, then you're well on your way to a good score on these questions.

13. A scientist is interested in observing a nova. Which of the following would she most likely use to view this?

   A. a telescope
   B. a periscope
   C. binoculars
   D. a microscope

Angela: This is more like a vocabulary question, because it hinges on whether or not you know what a nova is.

Willy: Maybe so, but it falls under the Technology banner. If you know that a nova is caused by an exploding star, the answer, A, becomes the most likely choice.

Strategy

Many Technology/Engineering questions ask you to choose the right tool for the job. Know basic tools (levers, wheels) and some scientific tools like microscopes, and you'll do fine.

That concludes a discussion of the S&T/E curriculum frameworks. There will be questions on charts and maps throughout the test—just answer them the same way you would answer Math chart questions. There will also be times on the open-response questions when your essay skills will come in handy. In other words, combine the techniques you have learned in previous sections with your basic knowledge of science and a healthy dose of common sense.

Overview: S&T/E Test Strategies

Strategy 1: Do the open-response questions after the multiple-choice questions, since they are more time consuming but account for less of your score.

Strategy 2: Since many more MCAS questions will ask about science than about technology, spend more time brushing up on science basics.

Strategy 3: While there is usually a precise, scientific explanation for the S&T questions, simply understanding the basic scientific principles and applying common sense often works just as well.

Strategy 4: Keep in mind the basics of conducting an experiment:

- Isolate one factor by keeping all other factors constant. That way, you'll have a basis upon which to compare any changes.

- The more relevant data you can collect, the better.

- For some experiments, using a control group allows you to judge the effects of an introduced variable.

Strategy 5: On Technology/Engineering questions, you may be asked to select the right tool for a job. Know basic tools (levers, wheels) and some scientific tools like microscopes, and you'll do fine.

Chapter 6

History and Social Science

Session Leader: Daniel Bryant

O Herodotan One, we started a bit late for our sixth meeting. We were going to meet at the downtown library, but it turns out that last year Daniel had volunteered to "improve" its fire extinguishers, and after the "foam incident," he was asked to not set foot inside the library again. Fortunately, there was a coffee shop across the street, and while the rest of the group drank hibiscus tea—a hideous concoction—I was able to munch on some Styrofoam cups.
—X!Frumious

NAME: Daniel Bryant

ADDITIONAL NOTES: While taking standardized tests remains his hobby of choice, Daniel is also an enthusiast of history. This has helped him win the "Most Accurate Yet Obscure Costume" prize at Eastbury's Halloween party for several years. Recent costumes have included: Millard Fillmore, 13th President of the United States; renowned Roman statesman Pliny the Elder; and hallowed French physicist Marie Curie. Daniel has watched all the documentaries produced by Ken Burns so often that he can now quote large passages about the Civil War from memory.

Ridley: So what exactly did you do to those fire extinguishers, Daniel?

Daniel: Well, I did refill them for free, something the librarians tend to forget when they discuss the Flaming Biographies incident. But I guess I also accidentally increased their "firing range," so when Ms. Baba used one, the foam shot out about 50 feet. I guess she wasn't quite expecting that.

Angela: That story is certainly one for the history books.

Daniel: Speaking of history . . .

Like its MCAS siblings, the H&SS test is given in three sessions. The test breakdown is as follows:

Angela: That sounds familiar.

Overview: History and Social Science

Format	Three sessions, each about 45 minutes
Number of questions	• 34 multiple-choice questions (1 point each)
	• 5 open-response questions (0–4 points each)

Daniel: Yes, in fact, you'll see that you can use many of the same strategies on H&SS that you used on other MCAS tests. Here are some of them:

1. As was the case on the *S&T/E* test, you won't need to know the exact historical (or scientific) fact in order to get a problem right.

2. As you did on the *Math* test, you'll use basic strategies to read and analyze charts and graphs.

3. As you did on the *ELA* test, you'll apply your essay/writing skills to some of the open-response questions.

4. As was the case on all of the MCAS tests, *Process of Elimination* is still your friend.

Now that I told you of the similarities, let me mention an important difference H&SS has with the other tests. While POE is useful on the H&SS test, you'll need some knowledge of history. This is similar to the Science MCAS, but since most of us know something about basic scientific phenomena like sunlight and electricity, you could get through the science questions with relative ease. This isn't the case here—some of us have no idea who wrote the Bill of Rights, and no amount of everyday experience will help us to bridge that gap. I call this Daniel's Rule of MCAS History: In order to do well on the H&SS MCAS, you have to know the difference between *George Washington*, *George Clooney*, and *Curious George*, the lovable monkey.

> O Brachiating Poobah, as a being from another planet, I didn't know the difference between these three individuals, and believe me, it caused me trouble. I kept watching reruns of ER, hoping to see a monkey perform surgery.

You have to have a good grasp of the basics, and then you can use POE and other techniques to get the right answer. Like the other sections, the open-ended H&SS questions take a lot of time, and combined account for only about one-third of your final test grade, so do them last.

The H&SS MCAS is designed to test students in four major skill areas, as outlined by the Massachusetts History and Social Science Curriculum Framework. According to the Department of Education, these four standards are: *history*, *geography*, *economics*, and *civics & government*. Here's a breakdown by question type:

Overview: MCAS History and Social Science Standards	
Standards	**Percentage of Questions on the Test**
U.S. History	44% of test
World History	22% of test
Geography	13% of test
Economics	11% of test
Civics & Government	10% of test

Daniel: It doesn't take a math guru like Ridley to figure what's important on this test: Focus your studying on U.S. history, since it is almost half of the test.

In fact, knowing U.S. history can help you on more than just 44 percent of the questions, since some of the Geography, Economics, and Civics & Government questions require knowledge of U.S. history as well.

X!Frumious: What exactly do you mean?

Daniel: Well, a geography question might ask you to pick the correct shape of the United States in 1845. You would have to know enough about U.S. history to know where the western boundary of the country was at that time. So while that question falls under the geography banner, it also includes some history.

Ridley: In many ways, the U.S. emphasis makes perfect sense. I mean, it's the *Massachusetts* Comprehensive Assessment System, not the *United Nations* Comprehensive Assessment System.

Daniel: That's one way to put it. Since U.S. History so important, let's jump right into it, shall we?

U.S. History

Daniel: While this is rather broad category, the MDOE does separate it into five core topics:

Core U.S. History Topics

1. Early America and the Americans
   (Beginnings to 1650)

   basic information about the Native Americans who lived here before the European settlers came

2. Settlements, Colonies, and
   Emerging American Identity
   (1600 to 1763)

   general information about how the first settlers lived

3. The American Revolution:
   Creating a New Identity
   (1750 to 1815)

   events in our war for independence

4. Expansion, Reform, and
   Economic Growth
   (1800 to 1861)

   major waves of immigration in the 1800s, and the push for women's rights

5. The Civil War and Reconstruction
   (1850 to 1887)

   names, places, events, and causes of the Civil War

Ridley: Hey, where's the 20th century?

Daniel: It's not an issue on the H&SS MCAS. You'll only be tested on events that took place through the late 1800s.

This allows us to narrow down our area of study by quite a bit. In fact, we can narrow it down even further if you think about the two wars, the *American Revolution* and the *Civil War*, each of which is its own core topic.

Information

The most recent event that will be quizzed on the H&SS MCAS happened over 111 years ago.

Angela: Why the emphasis on wars? That's seems a little violent.

Daniel: Granted, wars are not pleasant, but when you think about our country, those two events have had a huge impact on our history. Let's look at a sample question:

1. Which of the following countries was the biggest ally of the American colonies during the American Revolution?

   A. France
   B. England
   C. Mexico
   D. Spain

If you know anything about the American Revolution, you should be able to cross out B. After that, you need to have the basic knowledge about that war to know that France was our biggest ally.

Let's say you knew the basic fact that France was our biggest ally. Here's a way to use that knowledge on a tougher problem.

2. Which of the following individuals was a great ally of the United States?

   A. General Cornwallis
   B. Marquis de Lafayette
   C. Benedict Arnold
   D. Juan Velasquez

Which answer choice has the French name?

Willy: B, and since I know that France was our greatest ally, I should pick B.

Daniel: Correct. Here's an open-response question.

3. Explain how two of the following were important to the outcome of the Civil War.

   a. The industrial production of the North
   b. Ulysses S. Grant
   c. The Emancipation Proclamation
   d. The Union blockade of the South

Here, you would have to know enough about the Civil War to discuss two of these events. If you do, the question is fairly simple, provided you write out your thoughts effectively.

X!Frumious: What about the other U.S. History topics? You know, 1, 2, and 4?

Questions in those categories are not as specific. For example:

4. What did many Native Americans live in before the European settlers arrived?

   A. stone houses
   B. caves
   C. dwellings made of wood or animal skin
   D. tree houses

Daniel: The answer is C, dwellings made of wood or animal skin. For these topics, more general, less specific, knowledge should be enough for you to score well.

World History

Daniel: World History is also divided into smaller core topics. If you have enough general knowledge about these topics, then POE should take you the rest of the way.

5. Before ancient craftsmen learned how to make tools and weapons from iron, they were made of bronze. What is one advantage of using iron instead of bronze for tools and weapons?

   A. the melting point of iron is lower than that of copper
   B. iron is a much harder metal than bronze
   C. iron is much easier to shape than bronze
   D. iron is less likely to rust than bronze

Core World History Topics

1. **Human Beginnings and Early Civilizations (Prehistory–1000 B.C.)** *life in the early years of Man (primitive stone tools, no large civilizations, tribal living)*

2. **Classical Civilization of the Ancient World (1000 B.C.–500 A.D.)** *ancient societies of Rome, Greece, and Egypt, and how those societies still affect us today*

3. **Growth of Agricultural and Commercial Civilizations (500–1500)** *the Byzantine Empire, the rise of Islam, and other events like the Crusades*

Willy: Really, I don't need to know about *ancient* times to know that you would want to have the strongest tools possible. I would guess B.

Daniel: Common sense saves the day again. For questions dealing with ancient societies, you need to have some idea of what those societies were famous for. For instance, the Egyptians were masters of irrigation and farming, and built a society strong enough to create huge pyramids from human effort alone. (Granted, it was forced human labor.)

6. Pick one of the following and discuss how the Greek culture can still be seen in the United States today.

   a. politics
   b. philosophy
   c. literature

Strategy

Familiarize yourself with the famous accomplishments of the Greeks, Romans, and Egyptians.

We live in a democracy, an idea that had its beginnings in ancient Athens. So if you write about how the Greeks implemented democracy, and how it's used today, this question is yours for the taking.

Geography

Daniel: This is mostly U.S. geography, so don't worry about being asked to "locate the city of N'Djamena on the map below." In fact, these geography questions are not concerned with things as small as cities, or even states. Just brush up on your knowledge of broad regions, such as the *Sun Belt* or the *Breadbasket*.

Information

Geography questions on the test focus on the United States. Brush up on how the various regions are characterized, such as the Sun Belt or the Breadbasket.

Ridley: Where's the *Breadbasket*?

Daniel: It's the region that covers Kansas, Oklahoma, and Nebraska, since those states all grow vast amounts of wheat.

If the MDOE wanted to add a bit of history to a geography question, you might see this kind of question:

Use the map to answer question 7.

7. The shaded portion of the map shows the

A. Northwest Territory
B. Louisiana Purchase
C. Gadsden Purchase
D. Oregon Territory

Daniel: Geography alone won't get us this answer—we need to know some U.S. history.

Angela: Or, we could just use elimination and take a guess. I know where Louisiana and Oregon are, and since neither one is near the shaded area, I can cross out choices B and D. That leaves A and C, and since the shaded area is not in the northwest portion of the United States, I'll go with C.

Daniel: Right. President Polk would have been proud of you.

Economics

Daniel: Economics questions obey the law of *supply* and *demand*. If any of you has ever collected comic books, you should know a little about this. Prices go *up* when demand is greater than supply. Prices go *down* when supply exceeds demand.

So, if I have Honus Wagner's rookie baseball card, and nobody else does but everyone wants it, then *demand exceeds supply* and I can charge $50,000 for a piece of cardboard. But if I have 50 copies of Dane Iorg's rookie baseball card, which only my friend Tommy wants, then *supply exceeds demand* and I'll end up spending some Saturday gluing Dane Iorg cards to my trash can.

8. The Swine Flu epidemic of 1834 killed over half of the nation's pigs. As a result,

   A. more people went into pig farming.
   B. bacon prices in the United States increased.
   C. demand for bacon increased.
   D. pig farming ceased on the east coast.

Information

According to the law of supply and demand, prices go up when demand is greater than supply. Prices go down when supply exceeds demand. (This could be called "getting something cheaply because nobody really wants it.")

X!Frumious: Following the law of supply and demand, if supply drops greatly, but demand stays the same—I'm thinking of *ceteris paribum*—then demand will exceed supply and the price of bacon will increase, answer B.

Civics & Government

Daniel: The best approach to these questions is to brush up on the main branches of U.S. government, and to focus on studying about U.S. History, since that accounts for almost half of your score.

Ridley: I'm going to tell our Civics teacher Mr. Stone that you said that.

Strategy

Get to know the main branches of U.S. government.

Daniel: Until Mr. Stone is in charge of the H&SS MCAS and changes it to the *Civics & Some History MCAS*, I stand by my statement.

9. How many U.S. Supreme Court Justices are there?

   A. 7
   B. 8
   C. 9
   D. 10

If you don't know this, you could still use POE and rule out B and D as unlikely answer choices.

Angela: Why?

Daniel: Because 8 and 10 are even numbers, which means that the highest court in the country could find itself deadlocked on an issue. What would happen then? There would be no tie breaker. A and C are better guesses, and C is the answer.

And that's all there is to the History and Social Science MCAS.

Overview: H&SS Test Strategies

Strategy 1: Make sure you have some knowledge of history and social science. POE won't help you much if you don't first know the basics.

Strategy 2: Focus your studying on U.S. history, since it's almost half the test.

Strategy 3: Get to know the important names, places, and events of the American Revolution and the Civil War.

Strategy 4: Familiarize yourself with the famous accomplishments of the Greeks, Romans, and Egyptians.

Strategy 5: Get to know the main branches of U.S. government.

Epilogue

TO: X!Frumious the Explorer, currently stationed on Earth

FROM: The Most Supreme Ruler of the planet Kronhorst

RE: Your notes about the 8ᵗʰ Grade MCAS

Dear X!Frumious,

Having read your notes, I can easily remember why you are my favorite Kronhorstian. Thorough work! I learned a lot about standardized tests, and I am quite eager to try some of those tasty charcoal briquettes you were eating earlier.

Your study group notes convinced me to learn more about the MCAS on my own, so I used my human Internet connection and checked out the Massachusetts Department of Education Web site at **www.doe.mass.edu**. It contained a wealth of information concerning the MCAS as well as various other educational issues in Massachusetts.

I'm very eager to learn how well you do on the MCAS when you take it. However, regardless of what your score is, remember that this test is only one part of your educational career. Granted, it's an important part, but getting a low score doesn't mean you are a poor student. It might mean you had a bad day, or that you are a poor test taker, or that you need to brush up on some basic skills. So, if you don't do well on the test, I'll talk to the people who know your academic standing better than anyone else—your teachers at Eastbury High. They'll tell me how your scores relate to you as a student. Until I hear from them, though, I would not take your MCAS scores to mean anything more than how well you did on one set of standardized tests.

That's all for now. Come back to Kronhorst soon—Mrs. Supreme Ruler of the planet Kronhorst misses you, as do I. If you ever need any help tutoring, drop by the palace and we'll work on some test questions together.

Stay relaxed and do the best you can on the 8th Grade MCAS. That's all anyone can ask from you, including me. Well, gotta go—there's a planet to run, you know. I remain

        Your Loving Father,

        X!Frumious, Sr.

        X!Frumious, Sr.
        Supreme Ruler of Kronhorst, Most Scaly One, etc.

P. S. Why don't you bring your study group over for dinner sometime?